James Henry Chapin

The Creation And The Early Developments Of Society

James Henry Chapin

The Creation And The Early Developments Of Society

ISBN/EAN: 9783741152108

Manufactured in Europe, USA, Canada, Australia, Japa

Cover: Foto ©ninafisch / pixelio.de

Manufactured and distributed by brebook publishing software (www.brebook.com)

James Henry Chapin

The Creation And The Early Developments Of Society

AND THE

EARLY DEVELOPMENTS OF SOCIETY

BY

JAMES H. CHAPIN, PH. D.

PROFESSOR OF GEOLOGY AND MINERALOGY, ST. LAWRENCE UNIVERSITY

NEW YORK & LONDON
G. P. PUTNAM'S SONS
The Knickerbocker Press
1885

COPYRIGHT, 1880, BY G. P. PUTNAM'S SONS.

Press of
G. P. Putnam's Sons
New York

TO

MY CONGREGATION

IN

MERIDEN, CONNECTICUT,

AND TO

THE PROFESSORS AND STUDENTS IN ST. LAWRENCE
UNIVERSITY, CANTON, N. Y.,

WHO FIRST GAVE THESE LECTURES A PATIENT HEARING,

THIS VOLUME

Is Affectionately Inscribed.

PREFACE.

THIS little work is written in no spirit of controversy. It is not an attempt to *reconcile* Science and Religion. The author does not believe there is any *necessary* conflict between them, but that each has a realm of its own—each is capable of sustaining itself—and that, clearly interpreted, each may contribute something to the other, without invalidating its own premises or subverting its own conclusions.

He leaves the popular theories, therefore, to fall into line with each other or out of line, as the case may be, without any attempt to place a forced meaning on a word, or to draw any conclusions from scientific data that ascertained facts will not reasonably warrant.

He desires hereby to express his obligations to Rev. A. G. Gaines, D.D., President of St. Lawrence University, for valuable criticisms; to Rev. I. M. Atwood, D.D., of the Canton Theological School,

PREFACE.

who kindly examined a portion of his manuscript; to Profs. J. D. Dana and B. Silliman, of Yale College, and Prof. J. S. Newberry, of Columbia College, for personal favors received during the preparation of his book.

He has also availed himself of the published writings of Rev. Thomas Hill, D.D., late President of Harvard University; of Rev. F. H. Hedge, D.D., from whom the subject of one of these lectures is borrowed with the author's consent, and to Dr. J. W. Dawson, of McGill College, Montreal, though from the latter he differs somewhat widely on various points.

J. H. C.

MERIDEN, CONN.

CONTENTS.

CHAP.	PAGE
I.—PRIMEVAL CHAOS	1
II.—LIGHT	19
III.—THE FIRMAMENT, SEA, AND DRY LAND	37
IV.—PLANT LIFE	57
V.—ANIMAL LIFE	75
VI.—THE GEOLOGICAL RECORD	99
VII.—MAN	123
VIII.—PROBLEM OF CIVILIZATION	147
IX.—FAILURE OF PRIMEVAL SOCIETY	171
X.—DIVERSITY OF TONGUES	191
XI.—ANTIQUITY OF MAN	211
XII.—ANCIENT CIVILIZATION IN NORTH AMERICA	243

I.

PRIMEVAL CHAOS.

"In the beginning God created the heaven and the earth."

"Not to the domes, where crumbling arch and column
Attest the feebleness of mortal hand,
But to that fane, most catholic and solemn,
Which God hath planned."
—LONGFELLOW.

"The tokens of a central force,
O'erlap and move the universe;
The workings of the law whence springs
The rhythmic harmony of things,
Which shapes in earth the darkling spar,
And orbs in heaven the morning star."

1.

PRIMEVAL CHAOS.

THE world exists. Whence came it, and what was the order in which its several parts appeared? We live in the world and hold various relations to our fellow-men. *The subject stated.* How came these relations to exist, and what were the first steps toward the formation of society as it is to-day?

Such are the themes of our discourse in the Series of Lectures we now begin.

We assume the championship of no theory whatever — Scientific or Religious — but propose, with such helps as may be at command, to trace out what seems the most reasonable theory of the origin of the world, with its marvellous harmony and arrangements; and then, of the first few steps in the progress of human events out of which came social order and civil institutions.

For the sake of simplicity we shall, as far as may be, avoid the use of merely technical names and terms, and employ words in *Plan of treatment.*

common use. When for want of a convenient substitute it is necessary to use terms not entirely familiar, we shall turn aside from the line of discussion to explain them briefly, that when we proceed we may go on understandingly together. Two or three such words occur in the opening lecture, and others will appear from time to time.

So to our undertaking.

Sir Isaac Newton sat one day, it is said, examining a new artificial globe of superior design and workmanship, when an Atheistic friend with whom he had had frequent discussions entered the room, and after admiring the new globe asked the very natural question, "Who made it?" To which the philosopher replied, "Nobody; it happened." Such an answer to such question strikes us at once as not only unreasonable but absurd, and yet it is substantially the answer the Atheist must give to the question, "Who made the world?"

We are unable to account for the existence of anything having manifest marks of design, contrivance or adaptation of means to ends, except on the supposition that it was conceived and planned by intelligence and wrought into shape by skill and power.

The world created.

It will hardly satisfy any exacting mind to say that if there are sufficient causes in existence to produce a given result, that explains the result. It may explain the cause, it does not explain the occasion for the thing itself. If, passing by a field where a plough stands in the furrow, we are asked why such an implement was made, it is not sufficient to say, "The force in the blacksmith's arm and the skill of the worker in wood caused it to take form." It was *meant* for a specific purpose and constructed for a definite use.

And so our reason forces us back of the world to a cause beyond the world. Some Power beyond the world.

It is not within the range of our present purpose, however, to attempt to prove the existence of a Creator; but taking that for granted, to inquire by and through what processes the world was made to assume the form and nature which it has. We set out, hence, with the assumption stated in the opening of the book of Genesis, that "In the beginning God created the heavens and the earth."

If the earth was created, manifestly there was a time when it was not, and therefore a time when it began to be.

We do not attempt to fix the date of this event, or even to guess how long since the work began. For if we suppose it Date of the Creation but six thousand years since man appeared on the earth—a supposition for which there is no sufficient reason in Scripture or elsewhere — that does not help us to determine how long before that the process of world-making began. We can only say it was before all other recorded events, or as the Hebrew record states it, "In the beginning."

We do not attempt to dogmatize as to the meaning of the word "create." It sometimes means to *produce absolutely*, that is to originate — and sometimes to shape and set in order. In this passage it may include both meanings, both the originating of substance or material, and the shaping or setting in order, since, so far as we have any means of ascertaining, up to this time, space was tenantless and the universe was silent; an abysmal depth without an occupant. This, of course, we do not absolutely know, but back of that we have no record in nature or elsewhere.

The word create.

Hutton, a distinguished Scotch geologist of the last century, assumed that science had nothing to do with the *origin* of things, that it dealt only with existing causes, and that, therefore, anything beyond the range of causes now in operation was out of the reach of science. And on this theory he says: "In the economy of the world I find no traces of a beginning, no prospect of an end." This statement

Hutton's theory.

PRIMEVAL CHAOS. 7

is now regarded as too broad, for in the gradual change and wearing away of things, there is a prospect of an end, whatever may be said of the beginning. And the words already quoted give us our only starting-point: "In the beginning God created the heaven and the earth."

But it must be said of this account that it merely states the *fact*, without any attempt to explain the processes involved. And for this there was sufficient reason. It was important, in a religious point of view, that men should be persuaded that this world was the work of an intelligent and powerful Creator. The course and method of the work were of less concern. The *fact* is stated, but there is no clue whatever here to the processes.

The fact merely stated in Genesis.

If, now, we wish to know something of the processes by which the work of creation was wrought, we must turn to an entirely different field.

What, then, has Science to tell us of the origin of things.

The first condition in which science assumes to recognize the world is that of a vast nebula, embracing all the matter now contained in the solar system; and though it has been propounded, disputed, accepted, and then doubted again, the most reasonable and best at-

Theory of Science.

tested theory of the origin of the world, is that known as the nebular hypothesis. A nebula is a vaporous or filmy substance, more tenuous than the comet's tail, or the thinnest portions of the milky way. Tyndall not inaptly terms it "stardust," and Herschell more accurately describes it as "an impalpable haze," as it has no more appearance of solidity or substance than the most delicate or subtile cloud.

The nebular hypothesis may be briefly indicated thus: If we sweep the heavens with a telescope, on any clear night, we may observe nebulæ at frequent intervals; some having the appearance merely of a very tenuous cloud, others with a small nucleus at the centre, surrounded by a vaporous substance, denser near the centre, and thinning toward the edges, as if it were gradually condensing to a solid substance. Such bodies, larger or smaller, have inhabited the heavens during the whole period covered by history and tradition, and probably from the beginning until now. And each of the solid planets, like the earth, was once a nebula. Then, as to the origin of these several bodies, they were at first all one. Far back in the remotest ages, or in the very beginning, all the depths of space were filled with this impalpable substance. By the law of gravitation, it assumed

The nebular hypothesis.

a spherical form, as any substance will whose particles are free to move, as the tear upon the cheek, or the dewdrop on the grass, is round; and the whole mass had a rotary or whirling motion, for law and energy were already operating upon it. That is to say, it was not a chance agglomeration of waste atoms, rolling through space on a fruitless errand; it was the material of which this complete and wonderful world was to be constructed: it was intended for something, and to that end energy was put into it, and law controlled it from the first.

As this vast body wheeled on through space, portions of its bulk became detached from time to time, as water flies from the surface of a wheel in rapid motion; or, an exterior ring became detached, as the centrifugal force overcame the centripetal, and this ring first breaking up became aggregated in a single mass. And this process was repeated from time to time. However the separation may have taken place, the parts so detached not only continued the whirling or rotary motion, each on its own account, but received also an additional motion, dependent on the attraction of gravitation, which sent it in a circuit about the central mass. And from that time forth it had a separate existence, was a separate nebula, still retaining, however, something of the energy, and obeying the law that controlled it from the beginning.

How many of these lesser bodies were detached from time to time from the central mass, or whether the process still goes on, we have no certain means of knowing, nor is it of any consequence in the discussion that lies before us.

<small>Detached nebulæ.</small>

In process of time, however, the vast central body, or what remained of it, shapeless and dark at first, became the sun that gives us light and heat to-day—and one of the detached portions became the solid earth on which we live. Our first knowledge of the earth, then, so far as science is able to lead us back, is that of a nebula—a tenuous, cloudy mass, embracing in an intensely heated state, all the material that have since entered into the various forms of rock and air and soil and sea.

It may seem a marvellous thing that the solid substance of this earth could ever have been in the form of a cloud or vapor, not only the waters and the soils, but even the metallic ores, the iron and the gold, and the almost imperishable granite, flint, and trap. But we need not go far to prove that such a thing is possible. Take a piece of ice at dead of winter, and few things seem harder or more un-

<small>Analogy of Steam.</small>

yielding; subject it to heat, and it becomes a fluid, losing all its shape and hardness. Then put that water into the boiler of a locomotive, and as the train moves off, a white cloud streams away like a snowy banner. What is it? We call it steam. It is the same substance precisely that was ice an hour before, but no longer solid ice, or liquid water, it is a vapor. If, now, instead of allowing the steam to be dissipated in the air we could collect it in a cooling vessel, as we may from the spout of a tea-kettle, it would become water again, and if subjected again to cold, would assume the solid form in which we found it when we began our experiment. And thus it is proven that the substance, the material is the same, only different in form in these three states. And, now, what has been so often done with water, may be done with most if not all substances of which we have any knowledge.

Matter may exist in any of these forms, solid, liquid, or vapor. Iron may be melted, that is, changed from the solid to a liquid state. And, as in the case of ice changed to water, it needs only to be more highly heated to become a vapor. *Three forms of matter.*

And the same may be said, so far as experiment has been made, of all the materials of rock and ores that make up the substance of the earth

Hence we conclude that the nebula of which the earth was made embraced all these materials, so dissolved and attenuated by heat, there was no more density or apparent solidity than in the cloud that floats now against a summer sky. Rather unsubstantial material this may seem to make a world of, in which mankind are to live, create industries, and build their monuments. But so seems the steam as it streams away from the locomotive, but which in a very short time may be ice again.

That the earth was once heated far beyond its present temperature, is evident from the fact that many of the hardest rocks are simply cooled masses that were once in a state of mobility. It may still be seen how they boiled up and overflowed, and ran out in this direction and in that, like heated tar, till they cooled so as to preserve their shape. Also, melted matter, that on cooling assumes the character of rock, is still thrown out from the interior of the earth by volcanoes, so that the former fluid and heated condition of the earth is not a mere theory, it proves itself to everyone who has eyes to see.

Again, Astronomy tells us that our globe has *Conclusions from Astronomy.* the form at present, that of a sphere depressed at the poles, that would be taken by a mass in a fluent state subjected to such conditions.

And if the earth was once heated to a molten state, it only required a higher heat to reduce it to a gaseous, that is to say, a nebulous condition. And, therefore, the nebular theory of the origin and formation of the earth, is not only every way reasonable, but in good degree absolutely proven. Indeed Prof. Guyot, in a paper read in September, 1874, before the Evangelical Alliance in New York, stated that it had been demonstrated in an exhaustive mathematical calculation, by Prof. Alexander, of Princeton. Whether finally settled or not, this may at present be regarded as the theory of science, the one that best explains the known facts. *The accepted theory of Science.*

One thing more we must notice before we pass, to indicate the changes that came upon this nebula in its progress toward the completion of the world.

If the earth came originally from the sun, it must be that the material in the two are the same; and it has been one of the latest triumphs of science to prove this fact—that the material of which the sun is composed, and the substance of which the earth is made, are one and the same, and may, therefore, well have come from a common laboratory. *The earth and sun similar in composition.*

For a long time the sun defied all attempts to analyze its substance. We could survey its surface, and note its movements, but what its composition was, was a matter of pure conjecture. But the spectroscope now enables us to determine its substance, even more accurately than the telescope reveals its form and motions.

The Spectroscope. The spectroscope is an instrument invented some twenty years ago, by two German professors at Heidelberg.* It consists essentially of a series of prisms, and is used to determine the composition of a substance by the bright lines in its spectrum. Let us briefly explain. It has long been known that white light, as the clear light of the sun, is composed of seven colors—called the prismatic colors—so combined as to neutralize each other, producing white light. If a ray of sunlight be passed through a prism and thrown upon a screen, the colors are separated, and so separated are called the spectrum of the sun. A spectrum may also be produced by any other kind of light.

Spectrum analysis. It has been found further, that while a heated solid or liquid substance produces a continuous spectrum—that is, one in which the colors are closely matched together—that a heated gas or vapor produces a broken spectrum—that is, consisting of bright bands or lines of light, separated by dark intervening spaces.

* Professors Bunsen and Kirchoff, 1857.

PRIMEVAL CHAOS. 15

Of nearly seventy chemical elements* known to exist in nature, each produces a spectrum peculiar to itself, and therefore the composition of any substance may be determined, when reduced to a vapor, by the bright lines it yields in the spectrum, by the number of those lines, or by the order of their occurrence with reference to the dark spaces that intervene.

Now the sun produces all kinds of light. If, however, a vapor of any kind cross the path of the sun-ray—in other words, if the ray be made to pass through a gaseous substance—a dark band will appear in the spectrum, and in that part of it the color of which is produced by the like substance. That is the substance absorbs in one condition what it produces in another.

The application of spectrum analysis to the sun, therefore, is on this wise. It is observed, for instance, that burning sodium, the basis of common salt, produces a yellow flame, and that in the spectrum produced by such flame, the yellow assumes the form of a broad bright band in a particular position; and that in the solar spectrum this bright band is replaced by a dark

Spectrum analysis applied to the Sun.

---

* Prof. J. N. Lockyer, of London, on the strength of some recent experiments, ventures the suggestion that all the elements may yet be found reducible to the single element Hydrogen. The theory lacks confirmation, and seems as yet to command little or no confidence among scientific men.

band of corresponding proportions. Why is this? The matter is easily explained. Any element will absorb the kind of light it produces. If the color in the solar spectrum is absorbed, it must be by the same element that produces it. If the sodium band is absorbed—replaced by a dark band—it shows the presence of sodium in the sun.

The same rule holds good of other substances.*

Spectra of different substances. Thallium yields a green band; lithium a red band, with a thin orange one; hydrogen three bands, a red, a green, and a blue one. And so on, each holding in every case its own exact position. And these all have their corresponding bands in the spectrum of the sun; whence we are led, rather driven to the conclusion that all these substances exist in the sun, as they are known to exist in the earth.

Sun and Earth identical in substance. It is too much, as yet, to say all the elements found in one appear in the other, for investigation has not gone so far; the science is comparatively new. But sufficient has been learned to warrant the presumption that the earth and sun are identical in substance, and without any reasonable doubt had a common origin.

By this method of analysis we not only learn of what material the sun consists, but have also a very certain clue as to its condition.

* See lithographic chart (frontispiece).

PRIMEVAL CHAOS. 17

These elements show their colors only when heated. We must hence conclude that the sun, which shows all these colors so vividly, is in a highly heated state, even if we had not sufficient evidence of that fact from the light and heat that we obtain from the sun. These considerations, some of which are of quite recent development, are regarded in the scientific world as practically settling the matter that the earth was once a nebula that came from the sun. What, then, must have been its appearance at this early date? *[Condition of the Sun]*

It is easy to understand that when all space was filled with this vaporous substance, a dense darkness must have been in and over all—darkness was on the face of the deep, or the abyss, for as yet there was no sun or moon or star, as they exist to-day; and when the change had proceeded so far that both earth and sun had assumed definite forms and motions, even approaching a solid mass at centre, that still surrounded by a deep belt of vapor, steam, or cloud, there would be no light. Impenetrable darkness would hover over all, until by processes at first unknown, the conditions should be gradually modified and the original nebula pass upon that series of changes for which it was evidently destined, and through which it is passing still. We have to do in this discourse, however, merely with *the beginning*—that chaos out of which order came.

Conclusion.   So let us, in closing, mark well the correspondence between the theory of Science herein set forth and the opening sentences of the book of Genesis.

The one tells us of a nebulous mass, already yielding obedience to the plastic touch of energy and law, already preparing for a grand career of development into forms of usefulness and beauty, but enveloped still in deep clouds, a desolate and shapeless waste, incapable as yet, of supporting life. The other tells us that, "In the beginning God created the heaven and the earth, and the earth was without form, and void; and darkness was upon the face of the deep."

The correspondence could hardly be more striking or complete.

II.

LIGHT.

"Let there be light."

"Hail! holy light, offspring of heaven, first born,
Or of the eternal co-eternal beam."

"They say
The solid earth whereon we tread,
In tracts of fluent heat began."

"God said, 'Let there be light.'
Grim darkness felt his might,
And fled away;
The startled seas and mountains cold
Shone forth, all bright in blue and gold,
And cried, ''Tis day! 'Tis day!'"

II.

LIGHT.

IN the first lecture we collected the material of which to build the world, and so far as we were able determined its origin.

We are to speak now of the Origin of Light, with special reference to the time in the order of creative events at which it appeared. *The subject stated.*

If, to dispose of that matter at once, we turn to the account in the book of Genesis, we find these words in connection with the first mention of the subject: "The spirit of God moved upon the face of the waters. And God said, Let there be light; and there was light." Again, a brief, concise statement of the fact, without any attempt to explain the processes by which it was done. It is simply that the great and mighty one who evoked the completed world from chaos, did at this point cause light to appear. *The Hebrew record.*

It would not be in place here to speculate as to the precise meaning of the passage, "The spirit of God moved on the deep." The word translated spirit is sometimes rendered breath, and sometimes wind or breeze, so that there is opportunity for speculation, for such as have the time and disposition. / We prefer rather to regard the passage simply as a reverent recognition of the power and wisdom manifest in the changes that came by degrees over the dark abysmal depth, since these were not fortuitous happenings that might come to something or might come to nothing, but the systematic development of a plan devised and determined before the work began, and in which, therefore, every change and every movement contributed to the result intended from the first. And to express this idea in brief, no words could be more fitting than these, The Spirit of God moved upon the chaotic deep. It was the first beating of nature's pulse, "the first throbbing of her mighty heart."

Another mention is made of light farther on in this account. But there was reason for the wide separation of the two events, which will appear as we proceed. And with this brief statement of the ancient Hebrew record, we turn, as before, to an entirely different field of inquiry.

Origin of Light. What, then, has Science to teach us of the origin of light and date of its appearance.

First of all, let us keep in mind the substance with which we have to deal and of which we spoke in the preceding lecture. Chaos means confusion. The nebula was but a subtle vapor. As yet nothing had assumed definite form or character. There was the germ of worlds, but no world. There were the elements of water and air and light, while as yet there were none of these, none of the chemical combinations or mechanical unions so familiar to us now; and the various changes in nature that we know so well to-day, had not begun. There was absolutely nothing but the dark chaotic deep. But while it is possible to conceive of the original nebula as dark—for dark as well as luminous nebulæ still exist—we cannot suppose it continued long in absolute darkness, for one of the first effects of chemical action would be the production of light, though that light might be long obscured by overlying vapors.

We need not concern ourselves here with the nature of light—whether, according to the older physicists it is luminous matter radiated with immense velocity from the light-giving body or centre, or according to the more recent and probable theory that it is merely the undulations of a universally diffused ether. Either theory will answer our present purpose. *Nature of Light.*

For the sake of convenience in this discussion we shall speak of light as of two kinds, cosmic and solar; the first produced by chemical action in the nebula itself, the *Cosmic and Solar Light* other coming from the sun. This use of the term, "cosmic" may be open to criticism, but we use it for want of a better, meaning by it just what is stated, light caused by the nebula of the earth itself, after it was thrown off from the greater mass. It may, therefore, be called earth light or world light. While by solar light is meant that proceeding from the sun.

And now, going back to the point at which we left the incipient earth in the former lecture, let us carefully observe what changes came about. We deal now with the earth nebula, leaving for the time, all the others out of the account.

The earth a nebula. There is a dark nebulous mass, some two thousand times as great in diameter as the present earth, floating or wheeling its ample bulk through space.

The nebula changing. But as steam does not remain steam long after exposure to the air, but changes to a denser form occupying so much less space, so this vast vaporous body had not proceeded far in its course till the outer portions began to condense, or change toward a liquid and then a solid form, by which operation, of course, the mass was being continually reduced in size. The heavier particles gradually gathered toward the centre, forming the nucleus possibly of a solid globe, while the greater part still remained, a sort of cloudy envelop about it. But while the steam from the locomotive may change to a mist that we feel upon the face, or fall like scattered rain-drops on the ground, leaving their imprint in the dust, this nebula contains not merely water reduced to steam, but all the elements of all the material that now enter into rock and soil, in the form of a finely attenuated gas or vapor; and these are undergoing a change from their present to a more stable condition. The minute atoms of iron are uniting, forming larger particles; the atoms of lime are combining, and so on through a long list.

And as this process goes on a glow comes over the mass like the first faint dawnings of the day. The surface of the body is at white heat, and it gives forth a dim light. *(The earth lighting up.)*

But as the process still goes on, the gathered particles change to a clear red color. The surface is now red-hot, and lights up all the space around, and the earth has the appearance of a blazing star. To state it more concisely, the earth nebula *is* a blazing star.

This is what we have called cosmic light—not coming from the sun, but produced by the earth itself as it hung like a brilliant meteor in the sky. Something analagous to this may be easily witnessed.

Go into a blacksmith's shop, and heat a piece of iron as highly as can be done with a common bellows. It comes from the fire, of a whitish color, emitting an indistinct glow, not unlike the aurora or the dawn. Wait a moment, and at a different temperature it changes to red. It is red-hot, and will cast a glow of light far out into the night. Such was the change through which the earth nebula passed, from a dark, chaotic state, till it became a luminous body, shining with its own light. And it was by such means the fiat, "Let there be light," was first answered and obeyed.

Analogy of heated iron.

But now comes another important change.

To extend the foregoing illustration: if you observe the iron in the forge, from the brilliant and luminous condition of red heat, it soon changes to a dark color and becomes opaque, showing no light at all, any more than if it were cold iron, though it may still be somewhat hot. A similar change passed upon the earth; not immediately, for the larger the body the longer the time required in cooling. But in process of time the earth became dark again; for it had so far cooled, and the matter had so far condensed, that a thin crust had formed all around it, on the same principle that a slag will form on a pot of melted metal, though the interior may

The earth becomes opaque.

remain a long time after in a heated and even molten condition. A bed of fresh volcanic lava, also, will retain a perceptible degree of warmth for many years, varying according to its thickness and other modifying circumstances.

Thus we trace the series of changes through which the earth passed; from, first, a vast ball of vapor to a body of liquid or molten substance—emitting first the glow of white heat and then the light of red heat—and thence to a globe having a thin crust upon it, and so beginning to assume somewhat the appearance and character of the modern earth. As the process continued and the cooling went on, of course the crust grew thicker by degrees and more substantial, and thus was it fitted at length for the production and maintenance of life in its various forms. *The process reviewed.*

We are not yet prepared, however, to follow the earth in its development of soils and seas and rocks and rivers, for there are other matters that must be considered before we can present an intelligible view of the creation as a whole.

We have to do in this chapter especially with Light. We have spoken of light as of two kinds, and it is important that we keep in mind the distinction between the two. That already described as Cosmic Light, not *Distinctions of cosmic and solar light.*

light from a foreign body—not reflected light, but that produced in and by the earth itself in its progress from the nebula to the condition of a solid or encrusted globe.

We have now to speak of the other kind of light, of far more practical importance as it seems to us to-day—Solar Light, that coming from the sun.

It will readily occur to the reader, that if the nebula out of which the earth was made was originally from the sun, or if all the substance of sun and planets was once one nebulous mass, and if, as has been elsewhere stated, the substance of the earth and sun is the same, it is reasonable to suppose the sun would pass through a series of changes similar to those of the earth.

And that is even so.

As the earth was once nebulous and dark, so was the sun once nebulous and dark. "Darkness was upon the face of the deep" was as applicable to the sun as to the earth, though the passage quoted probably had reference only to the earth.

Analogies of sun and earth.

The analogy between the earth and sun may be traced still farther. As the earth, by the earlier condensation of its vapors became a glowing ball that shot out rays of light far into the depths of space, so did the sun by the same process precisely. And that condition, the condition in which it glows by its own light and sends its rays afar, is the condition in which the sun exists to-day; and by virtue of which it supplies light and heat, to what without it would be a dark if not a frozen world.

It required a much longer time for these changes to pass upon the sun than upon the earth, for the sun is more than twelve hundred thousand times larger than the earth; and the time required to work important changes bears some proportion to the bulk. But the great luminary passed its incipient period of darkness, then its dawn of white heat, and is now in the condition of the blazing star. *Changes less rapid in the sun.*

And so it will appear that the two kinds of light, designated as cosmic and solar, are the same in constitution; that is, are produced from like material and in the same way; by the combustion of elements that enter into sun and earth alike. And the two terms are used merely for the convenience of distinction. The period of cosmic light for the earth is long since passed. It closed with the first formation of a crust upon the globe, unless we except the tongues of flame that for a time shot up here and there through the rifted envelop. The light on which we now depend is borrowed from the sun. *Identity of cosmic and solar light.*

It must occur to the thoughtful reader at this
point, that as these changes are slowly
wrought, there must have been a considerable lapse of time between the appearance of cosmic light and that of solar light. A longer time was required for the sun to reach its highly luminous condition, by reason of its greater mass, to say nothing of the fact that the overlying vapors of the encrusted earth, as will be explained in the succeeding chapter, must have long obscured the solar rays, or prevented the free access of the sunlight to the earth.

<small>Interval between the two.</small>

It is worthy of particular remark that the Hebrew record so represents it; the one event being placed in the first day, the other upon the fourth. We have no means at command for any definite calculation of the period.

We might dilate to almost any extent, did it come within the purpose of this discussion, upon the office or uses of the sun; not only as the promoter of life and growth and organic change, but considered as dividing the light from the darkness, serving the purpose of a time-keeper. Without this provision we should have no definite and convenient measure of time. Without a definite chronology consecutive history would be hardly possible. And without history, transmitted experience would count

<small>Offices of the sun.</small>

for nothing in the economy of human life. Each generation would begin untutored by the past; there would be little or no progress, and any high degree of civilization would be beyond the reach of man.

The sun is not only a "luminary," but marks off "seasons, days, and years," and that with remarkable precision. He gives us now the light of day, and again leaves us in the darkness of the night. He brings, moreover, the seed-time and harvest, and the various seasons of the year, according as he is near or far, and his heat falls upon us in direct or slanting rays.

Such wonderful adaptation of means to ends, such accurate adjustment of the forces that still operate in the world, and such studious regard for the approaching needs of human life, may well command our devoutest admiration. For none of these offices of the sun, or the feebler service of the moon, seem to have been fortunate accidents, but essential parts of a complex, an elaborate, a divine economy.

<small>Adaptation and evident purpose.</small>

Two or three considerations, not belonging essentially to the history of the creation, but growing out of it, claim brief attention here because of their bearing on the general subject. We are proceeding on the supposition that the earth was once a nebula that came from the sun; that the sun and earth are, therefore, of one substance or composition; and that the sun is undergoing changes, similar to those that have already passed upon the earth.

Progress of our discussion. We have traced the history of the earth from the condition of a dark, chaotic mass to that of a glowing orb and then a blazing sphere, and then to that of an encrusted globe shining no longer by its own but by borrowed light.

We have traced the history of the sun from the same original condition, through the same series of changes, as far as that of the blazing orb that sends its light and heat afar.

The earth cooling off. Now, since the earth has passed through these several changes by reason of a cooling process, the radiation of its heat into space, the question arises, is the earth gradually cooling off, so that by and by it can no longer support life?

Yes; that is the plain and irresistible conclusion.

Have we any proof of this, aside from the deductions of a theory?

Yes. It is this.

Evidence from other planets. The other planets in our system, with their satellites, must have had the same origin as the earth; they have also like motions; and it is every way reasonable to suppose they are passing through similar changes.

And observation and experiment indicate that the planets Saturn and Jupiter, very much larger than the earth, are not yet wholly freed from their nebulous surroundings; whence we conclude they are still in a heated state.

Moreover, since the difference in gravity is much less than the difference in size, it must be these larger planets are so much less dense, and therefore so much less advanced in a geological sense than the earth. They are relatively "younger," that is, less mature than the earth. Not but that their origin may have been as remote, indeed more remote, since they are farther from the sun, but that their greater volume makes the longer time necessary to reach the same condition.

While on the other hand our moon, very much smaller than the earth, is already cold, through and through. A mere skeleton of a world, scarred with storms and gaping with craters of extinct volcanoes, but without any semblance of life. *Present condition of the moon.*

That is what the earth is coming to by and by; destined not to burn up, but to freeze out.

This may be a startling conclusion; though, when we reflect how many thousands of years the earth has already been inhabited, and that the crust as yet may not exceed a hundred miles in thickness, and that it must thicken possibly to four thousand miles before the internal fires are entirely out, it is clear there is no immediate occasion for alarm.

It will appear, then, that Mr. Hutton's statement quoted in the preceding lecture, that "Science finds no prospect of an end" of this world, was premature. It teaches us, on the contrary, that in the natural order of events an end must come at length to the existing order of things throughout the material universe. But it is not of the end but of the beginnings of the world we are especially to speak—the passing of this earth from the chaos and vacuity in which it began to a condition of order, harmony, usefulness, and life.

And so we return from this digression to mark, in closing, the point in the development of our subject to which the present discussion carries us.

The appearance of the sun is not yet reached in the regular order of events. We have spoken of it here for the sake of unifying our discussion of light, but the event itself occurred at a later period. It was after the establishment of the firmament—after the gathering of the waters into the sea—after the first appearance of dry land probably, that the sun-light struggled through the vapors that surrounded the sun upon the one hand and shrouded the earth upon the other.

Epoch of the sun's appearance.

Our present discussion takes us only to the first appearance of clear light, and that was not from the sun. The skilful chemist will show you now how, by the combination of certain simple elements, both light and heat may be produced. But this production was not dependent on man's invention or discovery. Far back in the line of ages, before there was a man upon the earth, aye before there was any solid earth or the sun in yonder heavens had begun to shine, the principle we now call chemical affinity, with gravitation and various forms of energy, were created and set at work; and out of the diffused and attenuated material that swung in chaos and disorder and black night, were gathering and assorting and combining the elements in due harmony and proportion. And in compliance with the divine plan, and in obedience to the fiat of the Eternal, "Let there be light," there was light.

> "Let there be light."

III.

THE FIRMAMENT,
SEA AND DRY LAND.

"And God made the firmament, and divided the waters that were under the firmament from the waters which were above the firmament."

> "The mountains huge appear
> Emergent, and their broad bare backs upheave
> Into the clouds, their tops ascend the sky.
> So high as heaved the tumid hills, so low
> Down sunk a hollow bottom, broad and deep,
> Capacious bed of waters."

III.

THE FIRMAMENT, AND THE GATHERING OF THE WATERS.

WE are now to speak of the establishment of the firmament, the gathering of the waters into the sea, and the first appearance of dry land. These events were next in order after the first formation of a crust upon the earth. It was the point, to all seeming, at which order began to reign. *The subject stated.*

The period of dark chaos was long past. The brooding spirit had evoked light from the gradually condensing nebula, and then the blazing star had given place to an opaque body bearing some resemblance to the earth as it exists to-day. *The situation.*

By these several changes the earth was gradually approaching the condition for which it was evidently intended from the first. There were no accidents, no mere fortunate happenings. They were parts, each in place, of the plan of the master mind that was over and in it all. And the forces, operating then and operating now, which we call electricity, gravitation, and the like, were of his creation and his appointment, and the obedient servants of his will.

After the breaking up of the original nebula into the several parts that now constitute the solar system, must have come a period of gradual separation. Even if we make no account of the force with which the parts were thrown off, but suppose each disjoined fragment, in turn, to have lain immediately without the slowly shrinking central nebula, there must have been gradually widening spaces between the parts successively thrown off. The centre of the earth from the centre of the sun is, in round numbers, ninety-three million miles. Mercury, thrown off later, lies at a less distance, while Jupiter, thrown off much earlier, is at a much greater distance.

The interspaces extended.

As these separated nebulæ condensed, or changed to a more compact form by the operation of gravity and radiation, the distances between them were increased, and so each planet came to have a space of its own in which to spin its daily round and make its annual revolution. These intervening spaces would seem thus to have been left unoccupied by any visible substance, making a vast expanse between sun and planet, and between one planet and another.

And here we approach what seems to have been in the mind of the writer in Genesis, when he penned the following words: "And God made the firmament, and divided the waters that were under the firmament from the waters that were above the firmament." *The record in Genesis.*

The word here translated "firmament" is from a verb that is said to mean primarily to "hammer out," or extend, as metal may be drawn out into a thin sheet, and alludes to the overarched and transparent appearance of the sky. But the word is also rendered "expanse" and sometimes "heavens," which means simply "heaved up." Neither of these words, as we use them, has a very definite meaning. We speak of the birds flying through the heavens, of the clouds floating in the heavens, and of the stars that fill the heavens. Of course there is no correspondence, actual or implied, between the height attained by the birds, the clouds, and the stars. And the word expanse is scarcely more definite, since it means merely an open space. *The word firmament.*

But if we substitute the word "expanse," in the passage quoted, for firmament, we shall get the idea more near the literal fact. For there is a separation of the water-producing cloud from the water-embracing sea, by the expanse of the atmosphere between.

But let us trace the process carefully from the time evaporation first began till the separation was complete. For that purpose we go back to the condition of the earth as we left it in the preceding lecture. It had just passed through the "ordeal by fire." From a blazing meteor in the sky it had so far cooled as to assume a nearly opaque form with a thin crust surrounding it for the first time. But the heat within was still so great that the crust was seamed and rent at a thousand points, whence issued jets of steam and tongues of flame, and sometimes streams of liquid matter.

The process traced.

In consequence, the atmosphere, or the region about the earth now occupied by the atmosphere, was full of various vapors. The waters when formed could not remain water, for the great heat immediately reduced them to steam. The steam went aloft, formed into clouds—fell in torrents of rain upon the hissing hot surface only to be immediately revaporized and rise again in a continual round; and thus the earth lay imbedded in a sort of perpetual London fog.

But as the process continued and the crust grew firmer, the outbreaks from within became less frequent. And the crust gradually thickening and cooling, the revaporizing became less general. The waters falling in rain found here and there a spot cool enough to remain upon, and thus by degrees the atmosphere was cleared of vapors. The clouds rose above, the seas settled beneath, and in process of time, the waters that were above the expanse were separated from the waters that were under the expanse.

We should here recall the fact, which has before been stated, that the earth nebula contained all the material since gathered into the various forms that nature assumes in rock and soil and sea. And while the process just described was going on, the heavier substances tended to sink and gather toward the centre, or at least to remain within the crust or flow over the surface in volcanic vents, while the more volatile substances, including the various gases with which we are familiar to-day, rose and mingled in the vaporous surroundings. *Substance of the nebula.*

And we shall find, as we proceed with our discussion, that an important consideration in the preparation of the earth was the clearing of the atmosphere of these noxious vapors. Open a gas-jet in your room; the gas mingles with the air, without changing its appearance to the eye, but so far changing its character as to make it first offensive to the smell, and then oppressive to the lungs. Now, this early atmosphere that which enveloped the forming *The atmosphere clearing.*

earth, must have been full of such poisonous gases; for they existed, had not yet been absorbed or compacted into solid material, and by reason of their volatility must have mingled freely with the air. Besides, we find the atmosphere about the craters of volcanoes of this noxious and oppressive character to-day as much perhaps as it ever was.

There was another end to be gained by this clearing of the atmosphere, first of mists and then of volcanic vapors, besides the dividing of the waters that were above from those that were beneath.

The world was being prepared for the abode of life. As yet no form of life could exist upon the earth, by reason, first of the heat, and second of the poisonous air. But the way was preparing, for to that end was the world created. Not merely as a wonderful experiment with nebulous matter, but for the abode and happiness of man. Toward this result had all the energies involved in the creation been manifestly working from the first. And, certainly, nothing in the whole progress of events went farther to fit the earth for the maintenance of life, than the establishment of a clear atmosphere between the clouds above and the seas beneath.

We pass now to a consideration of the second topic embraced in the subject of the lecture: the gathering of the waters into the sea and the consequent appearing of dry land. *Origin of sea and dry land.*

After the clearing of the expanse about the earth, it seems, to our common conception, to have assumed at once a more definite and independent character than it had ever had before. It now had the appearance for the first time of a solid globe swinging in open space. But it must be kept in mind that the crust as yet was comparatively thin, and liable to rupture at frequent intervals by the operation of the giant forces as yet untamed within. Geologists sometimes speak of the earth as passing through an "ordeal by fire," as described in the last lecture, and then through an "ordeal by water."

The latter came about in this way.

When the crust had so far cooled as to permit water to lie upon it, without being immediately converted into steam, the waters that now constitute the sea must have covered the whole surface of the earth. *The ordeal by water.* For the surface, as yet, was comparatively smooth, and there was no cause for the water to stand in one place or flow in one direction rather than in another. There was, therefore, no dry land. All was sea. But this was not to continue. The imprisoned forces kept in action by the heat within the crust, here and there broke their bounds, burst through to the surface. And as the volcanic matter ran out, the water very likely ran in, causing great explosions. We have an example of the kind in comparatively recent history.

A submarine volcano broke out in the bed of the Mediterranean Sea, not far from Mount Ætna, and for a time there was a lively contest between the fires within and the waters without. But the sea seemed to have most resources at command and quenched at length the volcanic flames.

Submarine ruptures.

But these explosions in the early crust were to work important changes in the surface of the earth; changes that in modified form and degree are still going on.

Around the opening formed in the crust the exuded material gathered till it rose quite above the general level, as some volcanoes do at the present day. Mount Vesuvius is little, if anything, more than an accumulation of material ejected from the interior through its own crater; a refuse heap of volcanic matter.

Besides, water was working in another way than that of merely irritating or antagonizing the volcanic forces.

The seas, which at this time covered the whole surface of the globe, loaded with corrosive acids, began at once to eat into and grind away the crust. *Corrosive action of water.*

And the waters as they flowed, bore along the fine dust thus formed till it lodged against the incipient mountain about the volcanic rim, or some other obstruction that presented itself, and there settled as a fine mud; and warmed by the crust beneath, and pressed down by the weight of waters above, gradually hardened, till it became a part of the rock or crust again. This was the beginning of sedimentary rocks, that now form much the greater portion of the rocks open to the investigation of the geologist. *Erosion by currents.*

And as this operation was continually repeated —the acids continually corroding the surface, and the sea continually wearing it away, and the waters continually carrying the loose and fine material till it found a lodgment—the surface was steadily growing more and more uneven.

We may suppose that wherever there was a volcanic vent made by the imprisoned forces, with the outflow cooling round it and the sweepings of the ocean heaped upon it, or against it, there was the beginning of a hill or mountain that might rise to considerable height or spread over a wide extent, according to the time occupied and the energy with which the forces operated.

<small>Other modifying agencies.</small> But it was not in this way that the principal inequalities were made on the surface of the earth. The highest mountains are not made up of volcanic matter ejected from vents within themselves, much less are great mountain chains of this specific character. In other words volcanoes are not the chief mountain builders.—We must seek some other explanation. And fortunately it is not hard to find.

As the crust thickened, and so opposed a greater resistance to the action of the internal heat, the outbreaks became less frequent; but the seething, boiling sea of liquid fire within was active and potent as ever, and sometimes operated with such tremendous energy, that while not breaking through, it caused a grand uplift of a wide area of the surface. And as we may readily understand, if there was an elevation of the crust in one place, there would be a corresponding depression or subsidence in another, usually in the immediate vicinity. And in this way the "high places and low places of the earth" were formed. The waters, which till now had spread the whole surface over, gathered by their own weight into the "low places" and formed the seas, and the dry land appeared.

THE FIRMAMENT, ETC.

That this theory of the elevation and subsidence of portions of the earth's crust is not *mere* theory is sufficiently proven by the fact that the same operation is going on, to a limited extent, to-day.

At the old town of Pozzuoli, on the shore of the Bay of Naples, a few miles distant only from Mount Vesuvius, stand several marble columns on a marble pavement of what was once a pagan temple, built probably before the time of Christ. [Temple of Jupiter Serapis.] The temple was built on dry land; but the floor or pavement is now nine feet under the water of the Mediterranean Sea. Moreover, the columns show by marks upon them, that they have been submerged to the height of twenty-three feet. Whence we infer that the land there subsided or sank to that depth and has since risen again. Indeed it is apparent within the past seven years that there is still an upward movement, and it is by no means improbable that it may by and by, regain its former level. Such oscillations, or alternate elevations and subsidences are by no means rare or unfrequent in volcanic regions. And such movements, on a larger scale, are perceptible on some continental borders, though the rate of progress is usually very slow. We mark this, then, as one of the efficient causes of diversities in the surface of the earth.

Since we touch here upon it we may as well dispose at once of the subject of mountain making, or of the vast inequalities of surface between the mountain tops and the bottom of the sea.

Mountain making.

When the crust first formed upon the earth, it was a larger body than after the condensation had proceeded farther, and many of the gases had escaped or entered into solid forms; and therefore the crust was larger at first, and afterward shrunk to meet the changed requirements of the case. By this shrinking the crust or envelop became wrinkled; sunk here into a deep trough, and rose there in a huge fold that we call a mountain chain.

A roast apple as it comes from the oven is plump and smooth, but as it cools the inside shrinks and the skin is wrinkled. A very similar operation occurred in the earth as it changed from a highly heated state to a condition in which the crust, at least, was cool. And mountain ranges are often nothing more nor less than folds in the crust, wrinkles on the surface of the earth.

If this cause seems inadequate to produce such effects, we have only to consider the height of mountains in comparison with the diameter of the earth. The highest mountains rise less than six miles above the level of the sea. The diameter of the earth is, in round numbers, eight thousand miles. Upon an artificial globe two feet in diameter a corresponding elevation would not exceed the thickness of common writing-paper.

Another cause of mountain making, of which some authors make much account, is due to the gradual accumulation of material along a certain line or trough till the pressure becomes so great as to rupture the crust, when the surface layers are squeezed together with such tremendous force as to cause them to assume a crumpled and folded position. Such is supposed to have been the origin of that portion of the Appalachian chain which includes the coal measures of Pennsylvania. *Folding by lateral pressure.*

Here our discussion might properly end.

But since we refer from time to time to the Hebrew record in the book of Genesis, and note points of correspondence between that and the theory we are developing from independent sources, we may fairly be required to offer some reasonable interpretation of the oft-recurring word "day," which we find in the passage, "The evening and the morning were the first day," or, as it is more accurately rendered, "There was evening, there was morning, day one," and the half-dozen passages of like import that occur in this primeval account of the creation. *The term day in the Hebrew record.*

No other word in the whole account has been

so much discussed, both by those who assert and those who deny the authenticity and value of the record.

The most obvious interpretation is, that it is a period of twenty-four hours—a solar day.

But the term is used without modification, in at least three different senses in this account: to indicate light as distinguished from darkness, without any reference to duration; then in the passages above named, and again to indicate the whole period of the creation. By no amount of ingenious construction can these three terms be interpreted alike. We must seek some other explanation.

No competent critic now, so far as we know, regards the term day in the recurring passages as representing a solar day, a period of twenty-four hours. There is nothing analogous in the actual work of the creation; besides, three days are recorded before the appearance of the sun, which alone measures and makes a solar day.

The attempt to correlate the "days" with certain periods of rock formations, as the Silurian, the Devonian, and so on, is equally futile, for there is no evidence in the rocks that there was any correspondence in point of time between these different formations. It is impracticable, then, to assign any definite limit to the term day in the Hebrew record, since it represents no exact or assignable duration.

What, then, may it be supposed to represent? Let us seek that which best explains the facts.

Premising that the passage, "There was evening, there was morning, day one," and the corresponding sentences, constitute merely a poetical refrain, closing the successive measures of the half-rhythmic account, Prof. Benjamin Pierce, some years ago, suggested an interpretation which has the merit of something more than ingenious novelty, though it may not precisely represent the primary meaning of the writer. *[Prof. Pierce's theory.]*

The theory is elaborated with some detail by Dr. Thomas Hill, in his "Natural Sources of Theology," namely, that the term is not a measure of time or space at all, but that the six days are "logical divisions in the survey of the universe," the logical order of thought in the mind of the author of the account. As if it were written "In the first place there was light; in the second place a firmament, with uplifted mountains and depressed ocean basins; in the next place plants appeared, and then the sun," and so on, following the record through to the end.

Viewed in this light, says Dr. Hill, "all the work of Ritter and Guyot, all the arguments of the

Bridgewater Treatises and the Graham Lectures are thus foretold in these brief sentences."

We go farther than Dr. Hill, and say the account not only sets forth the logical order of thought, but approximately the actual order of events.* Let us see.

1. The elements in chaotic darkness and confusion, followed by light resulting from chemical action.

Comparison of data.

2. The separation of the earth and heavens by an intervening firmament, together with the upheaval of mountains and corresponding depression of ocean beds.

3. The appearance of life in the form of vegetation, as will appear in the next lecture.

4. Appearance of the sun. If the theory developed in the second lecture be correct, this occurred at a somewhat advanced stage of the work. There was an extended lapse between the appearance of cosmic and solar light, though we have no means of calculating the actual or even probable length of the period.

5. Appearance of the animal world.

6. The appearance of man—and

7. If you please, rest *from the work of creating:* no additions having been made to the forms

---

* Dr. Hill regards this as one of the secondary meanings that may be found in the record in Genesis. It seems to us primary.

of life since the introduction of man. There is no intimation here of weariness, or exhausted power as some inconsiderately assume. The Supreme Spirit may be as active in guiding and preserving what he created as he was in the act of creating. The meaning is, simply, that at this point he ceased to introduce new types of life.

In what is usually called a second account of the creation, beginning at the fourth verse of the second chapter, the order of the first is reversed; that is to say, the order of time is not observed. The writer begins with man as the crown of the creation, and proceeds, in order, to those of less importance.

The reader is left to consider all the facts, together with the suggestions offered, and reach his own conclusion.

We return now from this digression, to mark, in closing, the point we reach in the development of our subject. We began *Conclusion.* with the earth as it emerged from the ordeal by fire to have a thin crust about it, but shrouded still in a bed of fog and noxious gases. We have traced its progress as the vaporous surroundings gradually cleared, and a wide expanse separated the clouds that were above from the seas that were beneath. We have traced it, also, as the crust thickened and volcanic vents gave rise to hills and mountains, here and there. And then, as the crust stiffened and grew stronger, so that it was not easily broken, the imprisoned forces, like raging, struggling giants, heaved it into huge folds here and depressed it into deep basins there, till the seas gathered into the deep places of the earth, and "the dry land appeared."

IV.

PLANT LIFE.

"Let the earth bring forth grass, the herb yielding seed, and the fruit-tree yielding fruit after his kind, whose seed is in itself."

"And then
The vacant hills did throb with life; and
The waiting fields put on parti-colored robes,
As for a bridal day."

IV.

THE VEGETABLE KINGDOM.

WE are to speak now of the world of plants.

In the preceding lectures we traced the development of the earth from the nebula, through the ordeal by fire, and the ordeal by water, till it assumed the character of a solid globe, or a globe with solid crust upon it, with continents outlined and seas confined within certain bounds; that is, through the inorganic and lifeless period.

As yet nothing had an organic form or constitution. There is no organism in the cloud or nebula. It may change form at any moment, and be still a cloud or nebula. There are no organic parts in the lava-bed or in the rocks that result from its cooling. A rock may be broken into fragments and each fragment be still a rock. And so in the creation, as far as we have traced it, nothing existed with organs and parts arranged in due order and proportion and for specific functions. *The inorganic period of the earth.*

We come now to the *organic* period, when

matter was organized for the introduction and sustenance of life. Organism implies life, and without organism there can be no life.

The organic period.

But before proceeding to that it will be expedient to notice certain changes that came over the "dry land" after it became dry, before it could support life.

The continent, as it emerged from the water, through diversities in the surface, was little more than a cinder, or at most a volcanic or igneous rock, somewhat like our trap-rock, but more like the beds of lava now found dried and hard on the sides of our volcanoes. Of course nothing could grow, take root, or find nourishment in this. But nature spends no idle moments, and the agencies of change were quickly at their work. There were the acids in the rain and in the air, so much more abundant than at present, as has been explained before, all tending to corrode the surface, which under the beatings of the storm and the continual agitation of the elements soon began to soften and crumble. The same process in a modified form may be witnessed to-day in the little vineyards and gardens of the peasants on the slopes of Mount Vesuvius, where the lava-bed is no sooner cooled than it begins to fray and the surface to disintegrate till a soil is formed in which the vine will take root and grow,

The processes of change.

Much of the material thus loosened, or set free, was borne off by the winds, or swept down by the floods and deposited at the bottom of the sea, to form the earliest bed of sedimentary rock, or possibly, by refluent wave, to be spread upon the beach again. But from these several causes there was a gradual accumulation of this material upon the land, which absorbing the moisture and distilling the subtle gases, at length formed beds of soil in preparation for the seeds and plants that were next in the order of creation.

And now, the earth being clothed with soil brings us to the first introduction of life upon it.

Whence came it?

There is nothing more certain than that there was a time when there was no life upon the earth. Equally certain is it that the earth is full of life to-day. We do not as yet know through what range of temperature some form of life may exist. Some plants will grow in water raised almost to the boiling point, while there is a minute fungus that flourishes amid polar snows, where the temperature is rarely above the freezing point. And still it is a conceded impossibility for life to have existed in the nebula, or in the molten condition of the earth preceding the formation of a crust. *[margin: Life in different temperatures.]*

Of the origin of life upon the earth, then, what

shall we say? The more general answer will be in substance this; that at this juncture in the progress of the world, the Creator, of his own purpose, in accordance with his own plan, and by his Almighty power, *created* the plants; that is, the germs out of which they severally grew.

<small>Origin of life.</small>

It has been suggested by Mr. Darwin, whose name and services entitle his opinion to much respect, that only a few germs were necessary to begin with, and after that, by the operation of natural causes, the growth went on from one form of life to another.

<small>Darwin's theory.</small>

But it matters really very little which view we take. Whether the original germs were few or many; whether placed in nature at one time or at different times, the absolute necessity for a first cause—a creator—lies back of it as much in one case as in the other. The question is not *how many* germs, or at *what time;* but whence came they—by whose appointment, and by what power?

And even if we venture on the bold suggestion of Tyndall, in his famous Belfast address, by which the equanimity of so many well-meaning people was disturbed, that "in matter he found the promise and potency of every form and quality of life," it yet remains to be explained *how* this potency came there? Who put

<small>Tyndall's suggestion.</small>

PLANT LIFE. 63

into matter the promise and potency of life? As the same author says on another occasion, "Granted the nebula and its potential life, the question whence came they remains to baffle and bewilder us."

This subject will be more fully considered in a subsequent lecture. For the present we content ourselves with the conclusions of some of the leading authorities in the scientific world, and those from whom a different verdict might have been expected, if one were tenable, that the origin of life from matter, by any inherent cause, is "contrary to experience and observation," and "against all the analogy of current nature."

We must look beyond nature, then, for the origin of life.

If before proceeding farther we turn to the book of Genesis for such light as it may give, we read, "And God said, let the earth bring forth grass, the herb yielding seed, and the fruit-tree yielding fruit after his kind, whose seed is in itself. *And it was so.*" Let us briefly analyze this simple statement. The term grass, as it occurs in ancient documents is not so specific as with us to-day, but is a general term for the simpler forms of vegetable life, or for a new and tender growth of any kind of plants. The word corn was once used in a similar way,

The cause beyond nature.

The Hebrew record.

and the usage is not yet obsolete—to indicate all kinds of grain. The sons of Jacob went down to Egypt to buy corn, when as yet the kind of grain now so designated was probably unknown.

With this distinction in mind we need be at no loss for a clear interpretation of the passage.

And now let us observe the very nice distinctions made in this first paragraph relating to life—and we are sure of none more ancient in all literature—between the organic and the inorganic world, and also between the different types of plants. "And the earth brought forth grass, and herb yielding seed." There is no seed in the rock or the gas, the nebula or the lava-bed, that you can plant and raise the like from. These belong to the inorganic world. But when matter was *organized* in the herb, then a seed was produced, which being planted yields the like again. Further: "And the tree yielding fruit after his kind, whose seed is in itself." The seed of the fruit-tree is in the fruit, and being planted will produce a tree of the same kind as that on which it grew. Such is the brief and simple, yet very comprehensive story.

What, now, may we learn of plant life from other sources?

The botanist will give us a far more elaborate statement, with a much longer list of plants, with their divisions and subdivisions. He will tell us of the cryptogams and phænogams, of the acrogens and exogens, of the angiosperms and gymnosperms, all of which terms have definite significations, and a place in any concise and complete history of plants. *Scientific analysis.* But we need not enter into all this detail. We require only a simple statement of the most obvious characteristics of plants, with such distinctions as will appear to the casual observer who may not be skilled in scientific lore.

First, a general division may be made into *flowerless* and *flowering* plants; a distinction that is easily marked at certain stages of growth. But that is hardly specific enough for our purpose. The following is more satisfactory, and for our use sufficiently exact, though the skilled botanist would require more detail.

Plants may be divided into three general classes, having special reference to their modes of growth.

First. Acrogens, sometimes though not very accurately styled "top-growers."*

Second. Endogens, distinguished as "inside growers."

Third. Exogens, or "outside growers."

---

* For the sake of simplicity and to avoid multiplying terms all the flowerless plants are here included under the single head of Acrogens.

The first class is of the simplest structure, with tissue chiefly cellular, and includes the sea-weeds, the mosses, the ferns, ground pines, and the like. These have generally an upward growth, flourish best in swampy and retired places, and seem to shun rather than seek the day, as if the sunlight were an intrusion upon their secluded existence. Moreover, they produce no seeds—only a spore, that is, a simple cellule, without the store of albumen and starch around it that makes up the perfect seed.

<small>Acrogens.</small>

The Endogens, "inside growers," are so called because their growth is wholly on the inside. They have no proper bark, distinct from the interior structure, and increase in size by pushing out the outer layers as additions of nutriment are made within. If we cut one of the plants across we shall find it is made up of a great number of separate fibres, imbedded in a sort of spongy substance, but with no indication of its term of growth. Familiar examples are the corn, rattan, and palm, the wayside weed and flowering garden plants. These differ from the first class not only in structure and mode of growth, but have distinctly-formed seeds. They are the "herbs bearing seeds."

<small>Endogens.</small>

The Exogens, or "outside growers," are so called because the additions in growth are made each season on the outside of the wood and immediately under the bark. If we take a transverse section of one of these, freshly cut, we shall be able to distinguish the divisions in the woody fibre which indicate successive years of growth, and thus to approximate at least, the age of the plant. Familiar examples of this class are the oak, apple, pine, and most fruit and nut-growing trees. *Exogens.*

What, now, of the order of succession in which these several classes of plants appeared?

It would be most natural to look first for those of simplest structure, the plan of nature almost uniformly being from the simple to the more complex. We should expect, then, first to find the Acrogens. The Exogen is accounted the highest type of plant. If, then, the Endogen is the intermediate, we should expect that to appear second in the order of time. It is not yet definitely settled, however, that it did so appear. The Exogen seems to have come as early, if not before it. *The rational order.*

But as the existence of Exogens implies a warm succeeded by a cold season—a time of growth succeeded by a time of comparative inaction—we may reasonably suppose, if the year was so divided so long ago, that the Endogens growing in summer may have *Uncertain conclusions.*

perished in the winter. Many of them are annual plants to-day. The growth of one year decays and disappears, and is succeeded the following season by an entire new growth. Therefore, the non-appearance of traces of Endogens in the earlier ages does not of necessity imply their non-existence at the time. We can only say, in such case, the record may not be complete.

But what are the indications from such record as we have? How are we to decide which type of plants came first, or if all appeared simultaneously?

Let us see.

In the various beds of rock built up on the earth's crust, since the dry land first ap-
<small>Testimony of the fossils.</small> peared and began to crumble and wash away into the sea to be there pressed and hardened into rocks, are found *fossils*—that is, remains of plants and animals that have lived and died. Sometimes it is a bone, sometimes a shell, and again a stem or leaf; sometimes with natural form still complete, but with substance assimilated to that of the rock; and again only an *impression* of its form remains.

In whatever stratum they are found geologists are in the habit of saying, " This plant, or this animal, lived and died when this rock was forming. When dead, it was swept by some current of wind or water into the bed of silt or sand then gathering at the bottom of the sea, lake, or river; that mud or sand, when in process of time it became rock, was its tomb; and when later the rock was unearthed and broken, the fossil appeared to give us hints of the types of life that existed on the earth so long ago."

Now, the fossil plants found earliest, or at the remotest period from the present, in the rocks, are all of the first or lowest class of plants, so far as it is possible to distinguish them, and chiefly if not wholly of the character of marine *algæ*, or sea-weeds. And it is quite certain that the earliest life of both plants and animals was in the sea. *Earliest plants, Marine Acrogens.*

The plants of simplest structure, and which we have designated as "top-growers," came first, in accordance with the theory above laid down. Then we must pass through a considerable depth of rock, coming toward the surface and representing, of course, a vast period of time, before we can certainly identify a single specimen of the higher types of plants.

The Acrogens increased in numbers, variety, and size with each succeeding age, covering the land at length and encroaching on the shallow margins of the sea. Among the ferns, of which a few species now crouch timidly in shady nooks, were those of great size and *Culmination of Acrogens.*

almost numberless varieties, and the club mosses attained the dimensions of forest trees. There were giants in those days in the world of plants.

The coal plants. In the coal period, the wide reaches of swampy land—for there were as yet few high lands—were covered with a deep, profuse, and tangled growth of stalwart plants chiefly of the first class, Acrogens. And it is to the vast accumulation of these, under long-continued heat and pressure, that we are indebted for the coal beds for which we now find so abundant use. The coal fields were stocked against a time of need; when the forests should fail in part and man be compelled to look elsewhere for material to keep his fires burning.

Condition of the early atmosphere. It has before been stated that at this early period the atmosphere was full of noxious gases. According to Prof. Tyndall, the air was so saturated with carbonic acid, that it obstructed radiation from the earth almost as effectually as a glass roof: the earth thus became a sort of conservatory or hot-house, and therefore plants grew to enormous size. But if this was the cause of the large growth of plants, it is evident that as the atmosphere cleared of this acid the plants must have appeared of reduced size. Not only so, but a radical change occurred in the character of the plant world. To the Acrogens were clearly added Endogens and Exogens, both of which were unknown in the earlier ages.

The change was not abrupt, but gradual—some types of exogenous plants appearing as far back as the coal period, or possibly the Devonian age; but it was not till comparatively recent times that the "outside growers," the oak, the elm, hickory, and the like became the chief features of the landscape. *(Appearance of the higher plants.)*

And so it appears, as far as the fossils enable us to decide, that the order of occurrence of the different classes of plants, were, *first*, those of simplest structure, flowerless and seedless; *second*, those producing flower and seed, and lastly, the fruit and nut-growing trees. In other words the testimony of the rocks bears out the theory suggested above, that the order of appearance of the different types of plants was from the lowest type and simplest structure to the higher and more complex.

We thus reach the conclusion of our topic proper. But one or two questions may arise which it will be well to answer lest they leave us in some confusion.

It has been said that the earlier plants rather shun than seek the sunlight. And if our theory of the gradual approach of the sun from a dark nebula to its present condition, as developed in a former lecture, be correct, *(Relation of sunlight to early vegetation.)*

the appearance of plants before the appearance of the sun is every way probable. The earlier plants required moisture and fed on matter dissolved by acids, of which there was great abundance, but did not to the same extent depend on light. And we are, therefore, warranted in assuming that in the order of the creation, plants may have appeared before the atmosphere was so far freed from clouds and vapors as that the sun appeared.

Another question follows.

Were all the *types* of plants introduced in this early and obscure period—the Acrogen, Endogen, and Exogen? By no means. The answer is readily inferred from what has been said before. By "the introduction of plant life" is meant simply the first appearance of any kind of plants upon the earth. The different types followed each other at somewhat uncertain intervals. The time cannot be definitely stated. We may not be able to determine the precise point at which any particular type made its first appearance. We can only judge by the period of its culmination, and that can be determined with little difficulty by reason of the abundant traces left in the rocks.

<small>First appearance of different types.</small>

The subject of plant life in the Hebrew record is disposed of in a single paragraph, for that account can be taken at best only as announcing in the fewest words the several divisions and important steps in the order of creation. We cannot suppose, however, the appearance of the different kinds of plants there briefly described, to have come in any single period of the world's history— only that at this point the first of plants appeared.

One point more, having some relation to the next lecture. Plant life is represented as preceding animal life. The truth is that fossil remains of animals are found as far back as those of plants. *Plants came before animals.* But there are good reasons for supposing them to have been a subsequent creation. Two or three reasons may be briefly stated.

1. Plants will thrive in an atmosphere too highly charged with noxious gases, and probably in water too highly heated, for the maintenance of animal life. And one office of early vegetation probably was to absorb the gases and clear the atmosphere for animal respiration. Plants can live where animals cannot.

2. Plants are the natural food of animals. Plants feed chiefly on inorganic matter; animals on organic. There are exceptions to this rule. Some plants consume organic matter. The mistletoe, indian-pipe, and other parasites derive their substance almost entirely from the plants to

which they are attached. A few plants also feed on animals. The Sundew for instance and the Venus'-flytrap capture insects and appropriate them to their own sustenance. But these exceptions are of comparatively small importance. It may be accepted as the general rule, that plants can live without animals; animals cannot thrive without plants. The conclusion follows, therefore, that the first appearance of plants came before that of animals. The animal kingdom was the later creation.

Still more conclusive reasons for this statement will be assigned when we come to read the geological record in the sixth lecture.

V.

ANIMAL LIFE.

"Let the waters bring forth abundantly the moving creature that hath life, and fowl that may fly above the earth in the open firmament of heaven. And . . . let the earth bring forth the living creature after his kind."

"See through this air, this ocean, and this earth,
All matter quick and bursting into birth.
Above, how high! progressive life may go!
Around, how wide! how deep extend below!"

V.

ANIMAL LIFE.

OUR subject is the Animal Kingdom.

In tracing the history of the creation thus far, it must be obvious to every one that the order has been constantly from a lower toward a higher condition. A notable illustration may be found in the change from inorganic nature to a state of organism and life. The same fact appeared in the last lecture in the history of plant life; beginning with plants of spongy texture and the simplest structure, passing through the herbs bearing flower and seeds, and culminating in the fruit and nut-growing trees. The orderly development thus traced will be found no less discernible in the animal kingdom. It is on such facts as these that Mr. Darwin and others base the doctrine of Evolution. *Progress in nature.*

And to the doctrine of Evolution, as the development of an order and the unfolding of a plan in nature, there can be no reasonable objection. We frankly confess it *The doctrine of Evolution.*

seems to us written on the face and stamped in the very nature of things.

But as Kingsley has well said, "If there has been an evolution there must have been an evolver." We cannot predicate or anticipate an order without an ordainer. There must have been an intelligent power back of it to devise the scheme and at least set the train on its way. We cannot conceive of harmony and order as a necessary or even possible outgrowth of chaos and blind confusion. With intelligence and power all else is possible; without these nothing is certain. And if we say *law* regulates and controls the processes in nature, the question merely changes form; whence came the law? Nothing is explained by the mere substitution of a word.

Moreover, it is not true, as some have assumed, that Darwin denies the existence of a Creator, as one or two passages from his published writings will sufficiently indicate. "To my mind," says he, "it accords better with what we know of the laws impressed on matter by the Creator, that the production and extinction of the past and present inhabitants of the world should have been due to secondary causes, than that each species has been independently created." And again, from his ORIGIN OF SPECIES: "There is grandeur in this view of life, with its

Darwin's theism.

several powers, having been originally breathed by the Creator into a few forms or into one; and that while this planet has gone cycling on according to the fixed laws of gravity, from so simple a beginning, endless forms, most beautiful and most wonderful, have been and are being evolved."

He has great faith, that *after life was started* on the earth there were sufficient causes in nature to bring out of it all the successive types and orders. He does not claim that this has been demonstrated or that it can be conclusively proven, on account of the great number of "missing links" in the chain of development. But he assumes that because these links cannot now be found, it does not, of necessity, follow that they never existed. That may be true. But until some clear traces of such links can be found the assumption that they ever existed is mere supposition or hypothesis and not established science.

<small>Causes in nature.</small>

Prof. Huxley, in his New York lectures in 1877, attached much importance to the series of fossils recently discovered in some of our western territories by Prof. O. C. Marsh, because, beginning with a remote resemblance to the horse, they gradually changed to a very close resemblance, and so went far to fill up a hitherto wide hiatus in the chain of development.

<small>Missing links.</small>

But if every break in the chain were filled, the question of the *origin* of life would still remain.

<small>Two questions involved.</small> There are, indeed, two separate questions involved:

First, the origin of life.

Second, the method of its transmission.

Prof. Mivart assumes, and we think rightly, that with the first, physical science has nothing to do, and is incompetent to deal. Nevertheless we are not forbidden to inquire.

There are two principal theories, with various modifications of each.

1. The germ theory; that is, that all life proceeds from an antecedent form of life—and which implies a creator.

2. The theory of spontaneous generation, that is, that life is evolved from dead matter, in certain conditions, without the aid or operation of anything beyond itself.

The latter theory is by no means new. Centuries ago it was believed that tadpoles were generated out of the mud along the borders of stagnant pools, by the vivifying action of the sun; caterpillars from the leaves on which they fed, and eels from the oozy slime of the Nile. And the hypothesis, in one form or another, has been revived or restated many times since the period of early Greek history.

The question has been very fully discussed recently, and with the aid of elaborate experiments, by Profs. Tyndall and H. C. Bastian, but with widely differing results. To reach any definite conclusion and make the test satisfactory it was agreed to take dead matter—isolate it from all contact with life—place it under favorable conditions for the development of life, if such thing were possible, and await the result. The experiment was a difficult one, but followed out with faithful detail by both experimenters. The material used was chiefly a liquid containing an infusion of hay, bits of cheese, or other organic substance. This was put in a bottle and brought to the boiling point, to destroy whatever germs it might contain—the bottle then hermetically sealed to protect the liquid from all possible contact with surrounding life, and left in a moderately warm temperature for several days. If at the end of the time the liquid showed signs of fermentation or putrefaction, it was taken as an indication of life; if no such signs appeared, it was regarded as absolutely sterile.

Spontaneous generation. (Tyndall and Bastian.)

A great number of tests were made. But the result, thus far, seems to have been to array these eminent authorities against each other; Bastian claiming to have demonstrated the fact, Tyndall to have disproved the theory.

It appeared at one time that the origin of life, in some of its forms at least, might be traced to a slime that covered the bottom of the deep seas, since specks of living matter were found in it. {Bathybius (Huxley and Hæckel).} The suggestion awakened much interest among scientific men, and Profs. Huxley and Hæckel in particular entered into a careful investigation. It afterward appeared that this slime occurs only in isolated sections of the sea-bottom — that oftener than otherwise it contains no life; and finally, by the microscopic investigations of Sir Lionel Beale, that this ooze or slime, instead of a bed of primitive life, is decaying matter out of which the life has not yet wholly perished. The living specks were the last of their generation rather than the first.

Indeed, there is little doubt that further investigation will prove the simple microscopic forms of life known as monad, bacteria, and the like, to be the result of decomposition of higher forms of life, rather than the beginnings of new life. The ooze at the bottom of ponds often shows traces of animal life, but it is decaying rather than primitive life. Instead of representing matter in the process of changing to the first form of life, it represents life in the last stages of decay, on the point of lapsing into the condition of dead matter.

Prof. Huxley, in his recent study of "The Crayfish," speaking of the wonderful changes that take place in the egg as it develops into the embryo animal, says they are "the necessary consequences of the interaction of the molecular forces resident in the substance of the impregnated ovum with the condition to which it is exposed," and compares it to the process of crystallization in minerals. But, aside from the fact that there is as yet an unbridged chasm between organic and inorganic substances—the one depending upon molecular stability and the other upon the exact opposite, molecular instability, or a constant change of atoms—the changes in crystallization are purely chemical. Does Prof. Huxley intend to be understood as regarding the changes in the egg as purely chemical? We think not; and if not, then the comparison fails. There is unquestionably some force or forces acting in the egg. But "the interaction of molecular forces" affords no explanation whatever. That operation needs explanation quite as much as the original process.

<small>Huxley's "The Crayfish."</small>

Again, after noting the close resemblance between the lowest forms of animals and plants, he proceeds: "Given, one of these protoplasmic bodies, of which we are unable to say whether it is plant or animal, and *endow it with such inherent capacities of self-modification* [the italics are our own] as are manifested under our eyes by developing ova, and we have a sufficient reason for the existence of any animal or any plant." But Prof. Huxley will surely concede that the assumption that matter is thus endowed, is *the very point to be proved*. And further, if such powers of modification are found in matter in some conditions, the question still remains, Whence came they? Are they due merely to conditions, or is there really an added force? Thus far it must be confessed the evidence is overwhelmingly in favor of the latter.

And so, after all this parley and delay, the scientific world is practically thrown back upon the Professor's own dictum in the "Encyclopedia Britannica," article *Biology*, that "of the causes which have led to the origination of living matter, we know absolutely nothing."

<small>Present attitude of science.</small>

The curious suggestion of Sir William Thompson, that life was imported to the earth by meteoric agency, need not detain us long, for it is but a suggestion at the best, with no pretence of proof; and if the fact were conceded, it would only push the question of origin a little farther back: it would explain nothing. For manifestly we can predicate nothing of meteoric matter that may not with equal propriety be predicated of the earth. If the meteor is a

<small>Meteoric origin of life.</small>

fragment of a decayed or disjointed world, how came life into that world? This attempt at explanation, if it is seriously intended as an explanation, leaves the inquirer just where it finds him.

A word, in passing, as to the development of one race of animals out of another. It must be said the like has never been witnessed, though many attempts have been made. In no case has one animal ever been known to produce an animal of a race or species essentially different from itself. And though Prof. Hæckel insists, with some show of impatience, that it is *unscientific* to demand such proof, considering the time required to produce essential variations, it is certainly quite as unreasonable to ask us to accept what it is confessed has never yet been proven. It is true that some modifications have been effected in animals under domestication, as shown by Mr. Darwin, but that is no argument for variation by "natural selection;" the one implies intelligent oversight, the other expressly disowns it. *[Possible development.]*

What, then, of the germ theory?

It is conceded on all hands that we have no certain knowledge of life produced otherwise than from some antecedent form of life. The plant springs from a seed which encloses a living germ. The offspring de- *[The germ theory.]*

scends from the parent through a series of changes beginning in a living cell.

All our knowledge and experience, then, are in favor of this theory.

But the existence of a living germ, whether one or more, with the possibility of definite development, implies the existence of a Creator with intelligence, power, will, and purpose. And, as before said, with so much conceded, all else follows easily.

To enter with more detail upon the various theories touching the origin and transmission of life would lead us quite outside the range of discussion contemplated in these pages, and we turn now, after so long a digression, to the immediate subject of the present lecture: The Animal Kingdom.

After the appearance of plants which might serve as food for animals, and after the atmosphere was so far cleared of poisonous gases as to adapt it for respiration, came a new order of existence, the animal creation, briefly epitomized in Genesis thus: "And God said, let the waters bring forth abundantly the moving creature that hath life, and fowl that may fly above the earth in the open firmament of heaven. And ... let the earth bring forth the living creature after his kind, cattle and creeping things and beasts of the earth ... and it was so."

[margin: The animal world.]

It is here stated that the water and the earth brought forth living things. But, as we have had occasion to note before, the narrative recognizes no fortuitous happening in this—no chance development or occurrence. It was according to the divine ordering of events. There the author finds, every time, his sure cause and sufficient starting-point. It was the Creator working by plain and definite methods, with intent to bring out of chaos the order, harmony, and beauty of a completed and peopled world.*

The Hebrew record.

* Since the above was written a notable work by R. W. Wright, entitled "*Life its True Genesis*," has appeared, in which the position is assumed and defended with much skill and labor that "the primordial germs (meaning germinal principles of life) of all living things, man alone excepted, are in themselves upon the earth, and that they severally make their appearance, each after its kind, whenever and wherever the necessary environing conditions exist." In these facts he finds the interpretation of the words, "Let the earth bring forth," etc. Not that the germs develop from the soil, according to evolution, but that they exist, were implanted in the earth, and that they not only may but must appear, whenever the necessary conditions occur. He illustrates by the alternations of forest trees and changes of vegetable growth, without the known presence of seeds, as the fire-weed appears in a burnt forest though it may not have been known within hundreds of miles before, plantain springs up about a new house, aconite about an alpine hut, and white clover instead of the native wild grasses, in a used pasture. On the same principle he would account for the *simultaneous* appearance of like flora, in widely remote sections of the earth. If we understand the author—we could wish he had been more explicit on this point—he would apply the same reasoning to the animal world, man alone excepted. The theory is a bold and somewhat novel one.

According to this record, the earliest life was in the sea. There is nothing definite as to form or quality, only that it was a "moving thing that had life," and was thus distinguished from the plant which is usually fixed, and that it "brought forth abundantly," or multiplied rapidly. The description is that of an animal of low grade or of the simplest structure. The next mention is of fowl, or what is deemed a more accurate rendering, "winged creatures," and must include the forms of life that are in the air. Allusion is next made again to life in the water under the general term "great whales," or reptiles.

And following this by so wide an interval as to be placed at the beginning of the following day, came "the beasts of the earth," including cattle and creeping things, or the animals in general that live on the land, as distinguished from those that live in the air or dwell in the sea.

Let us claim no more for this account than the language fully warrants. Life, first in the water, then in the air, then on the land. This is the order indicated, and we must suppose the order intended. Again, we are led to infer that the first forms of animal life were very simple, scarcely differing from plants, except that they were endowed with power to move, and that in process of time and with some orderly sequence, the line proceeded toward higher and more complex forms; to the fishes that inhabit the waters, the birds that people the air, the cattle that roam on the hills, and the beasts that prowl in the jungle.

This is, in brief, the story told us in Genesis of the creation and appearance of the animal world.

Let us now turn to other fields of inquiry with reference to the same things.

First, let us note what science teaches of the varieties of animal life, or the divisions of the animal kingdom as a whole. And then let us read in the rocks, as far as we are able, the order in which these several divisions made their first appearance. For it is on the fossils we must rely at last to know positively which came first and which came afterward. And fortunately, we shall find this an easier task than in the case of plants, especially in the earlier ages, as the remains are so much more abundant and more perfectly preserved in form. *Scientific analysis.*

We encounter a difficulty here in adopting a division of the animal kingdom that will be intelligible to all without extended explanation.

There are certain broad distinctions in the animal world that are useful in such discussions, as far as they go. There are the cold-blooded animals and the warm-blooded. There are the gill-breathers and the lung-breathers. But these *Different classifications.*

are not sufficiently specific for our purpose. A division was suggested by an eminent naturalist a few years ago, which for its simplicity we hoped might come into use. It was substantially this. Animals may be approximately classified thus:— 1. Those with stomachs. 2. Those with shells. 3. Those with legs or other limbs. 4. Those with heads. That is to say, these parts severally are the *specific characteristics* of the different groups. The lowest type of animal has little if any organism except a stomach. Then come those with stomachs, to be sure, but adding a shell for protection; or some type of limb for locomotion, whether on the ground, in the water, or in the air. While the most important part about the higher animal, as a distinctive type, is the head.

But this classification, while peculiarly suggestive, was not sufficiently specific for scientific work, and never came into use.

And there seems no resource left us but to turn to zoology, as in the last lecture to botany, and, simplifying the scientific terms as far as we may, adopt the classification there employed.

Naturalists recognize five divisions of the animal kingdom, namely:

<small>Zoological distinctions.</small> I. Protozoans; literally "first livers," generally microscopic, though sometimes attaining to considerable size.

II. Radiates, or star-shaped animals.

III. Mollusks, or soft-bodied animals, generally with shells.

IV. Articulates, having a jointed or ring-like structure.

V. Vertebrates, or animals with internal skeleton, including a vertebral column, or backbone.

All animals that live, and all of which we find any traces in the rocks, are of one of these classes. Let us examine the structure and mode of life of each. A single specimen of the first, the Protozoan, will answer our purpose.

The Amoeba, a minute animal sometimes found in stagnant pools, seems nothing but a bit of pulp. The outside is much like jelly; the inside somewhat granular. It has no limbs proper, and still it moves. It has no mouth, and still it eats. It will fasten on a seed, or other substance that will serve as food, no matter what part the seed touches first, and soon it will disappear inside the animal, and in due time the refuse is cast out in an equally mysterious way; the animal having absorbed whatever was nutritious, ejects what does not serve its purpose. This is a type of the animal with a stomach, the first essential in the living creature, and one that never looses its importance. Without a stomach that performs its functions well, there can be no sound

The Protozoan.

and healthy organism in any animal whether of high or low degree. The little animal just described will serve as an illustration of the simplest form of life, though the sponge is a more familiar example and one more easily examined.

Next come the Radiates, so called from their star-like form, which in addition to a stomach have a perceptible mouth. They have also rays or parts branching in all directions much like the leaves of a plant, which serve them in moving through the water or in gathering food.

<small>The Radiate.</small>

Among the best known examples of these are the star-fish, the jelly fish, and most corals. Their structure and habits are simple, but a considerable advance over the Protozoans.

Next in order come the Mollusks, including everything that wears a shell, either without or within, from the commonplace clam and oyster to the artistically formed ammonite and the delicately tinted nautilus, and from the slow-footed snail to the slimy and voracious cuttle-fish, which there is little doubt is the mysterious and dreaded sea-serpent of the modern seas.

<small>The Mollusk.</small>

The almost infinite variety that make up this branch of the animal world will appear on examination of any large collection of shells, such as natural history cabinets afford.

Most of these animals are included under the general name of "shell-fish." But they are in no proper sense fishes. They have no more similarity in structure or habit to the fish than to the seal or manatee, which also inhabit the sea.

And, now, does it occur to the reader that in all these classes of animals, Protozoans, Radiates, and Mollusks, there are scarcely any that live on dry land? The sea swarmed with life while as yet the land was destitute.

But let us go a little farther, and we shall find there were different orders of life in store.

The next division of the animal kingdom, the Articulates, having a ring-like or jointed structure, includes the lobster, which in place of shell has a closely articulated crust, together with the worms and all the insect world. This division has a few representatives in the sea, but takes us, for the most part, on to the land and into the air. It is unnecessary to cite particular examples. *The Articulate.*

Finally comes the division known as the Vertebrates, in which the animal kingdom culminates, or reaches its highest perfection. *The Vertebrate.*

Among the animals with backbones we shall find those that live in the water, those that live in the air, and those that live on the land. But it is a fact quite in accord with the principle already established, that that in the sea came first, that in the air followed, and then that on the land.

First the fishes, then the birds, then the beasts.

So much for what science teaches of the divisions and characteristics of the animal kingdom.

The question follows next, in what order did these several types of life appear, or was their appearance simultaneous? We pursue the same course as in dealing with plants in the last lecture. In the earliest rocks containing fossils of animals are found only Protozoans, "first livers" as they are appropriately styled on that account. The remains are few, as might be expected, for they are slight and simple in structure, and therefore perishable.

The order of succession.

Next we find, in rocks somewhat later, the remains of Radiates, especially corals, and Mollusks of almost infinite variety. Beds of limestone are often found consisting almost wholly of one or the other of these. In coral limestone, however, traces of the original skeletons are comparatively rare; they were broken and crushed in the process of consolidation; but in "shell-limestone" made up of the remains of mollusks, as that found near St. Augustine, Florida, the skeletons are often found almost as perfect as in the living animal.

The foregoing, it will be observed, comprise the

first three types of life above described. As we
proceed in our investigation, from the older toward
the more recent rock formations, we shall find
these several groups still, together with the Articulates, and the Vertebrates are also added, thus
completing the list of distinct types of animal life.
But the indications of an onward and upward progress in the forms of life do not cease here. Each
succeeding age witnesses a marked change in the
several groups or types of life. And this is particularly observable among Vertebrates.

First or lowest among vertebrated animals are
fishes. And to such rank did they attain at one
time, in point of numbers, variety, and size, that the
period has received the name of the Age of Fishes.
After this came an Age of Reptiles; the reptile
ranking above the fish in completeness of structure
and adaptedness to different conditions of life.
Then came the Age of Mammals, generally large
land animals. And finally the Age of Man, who
represents the highest class in the whole group of
vertebrated animals.

Such is the story, in brief, the rocks tell us of
the various types and classes of animals that have
lived and died upon the earth, together with the
order in which they succeeded one another.

How do we know such animals as these ever
lived? In the same way that if, digging in an

ancient cemetery, we came upon the skeleton of a very large man, we should know that a giant had sometime been buried there. We find the remains of them in the rocks that compose the crust of the earth. No such remains would appear had not such creatures lived. Nor would such relics have been embodied in the rocks, had they not lived and died at the time such rocks were in process of formation. But this will more fully appear in the succeeding lecture.

Testimony of the rocks.

And now the reader may be interested to know what points of correspondence clearly exist between the record just laid down and that which appears in Genesis. It would be idle to say we find in the latter a detailed history or complete analysis. The author was not writing a treatise on zoology. He, at most, indicates only the most obvious characteristics of different classes of animals, and that chiefly by the element in which they live. The order observed is this. First life—abundant life—in the sea, then life in the air, then life on the land.

Comparison of records.

We found by indications in the rocks that the sea abounded with life, while the land was destitute; then that there was probably life in the air, before any pertaining strictly to the land; and finally that "the beasts of the earth"—in other words, land animals, were the last to appear preceding the advent of man. These points will plainly appear to any one who choses to examine the records together.

The precise point at which each group or division of animals made its first appearance cannot be certainly determined—for, like the earliest plants, the earliest animals may have disappeared entirely, owing to the condition of the earth, its temperature and surroundings, and the volcanic convulsions that took place. But the time at which each rose into *prominence*, and became the leading feature or controlling power, can be determined with all the accuracy science can give, with the aid of the most abundant fossils.

And so we return to the point from which we started — that after the surface of the earth was divided into land and sea, and the hardened crust had worn and softened into beds of soil—after plants had had all the life to themselves awhile, and the air was so far purified it could be breathed; then, by the divine fiat, came forth in the waters the moving creature that had life, and winged creatures that fly above the earth; and then appeared on the land, cattle and creeping things and beasts of the earth, each after his kind.

And thus was the earth made ready, by long process of preparation, for the abode of intelligence and the use of man.

Conclusion.

VI.

Reading the Record.

"The invisible things of him are clearly seen, being understood by the things that are made."

"In contemplation of created things,
By steps we may ascend to God."
—MILTON.

"Nature hath made nothing so base, but can
Read some instruction to the wisest man."

"And in that rock are shapes of shells, and forms
Of creatures in old worlds,
Whose generations lived and died ere man
Appeared upon the scene."
—*Adapted from* CRABBE.

VI.

READING THE GEOLOGICAL RECORD.

WE propose in this discourse to see what kind of record geology can give us of life upon the earth.

To that end we must speak first of certain rock formations; whence the material comes, how it is deposited, and what changes follow. And as nature's methods are very constant, if we determine the processes for one age we solve the problem for all ages. *Formation of rocks.*

The formation of different kinds of rocks may be illustrated as follows. After a heavy rain, the water that flows along the streets of a country village, where the conditions of nature are but slightly changed, will be turbid and muddy; moving more or less rapidly according to the descent of the ground, and carrying along sand, clay, gravel, and such refuse as may come in its way. Moreover, if the surface be uneven and the soil soft or friable, the hillsides will be furrowed out and partially washed away. As the rivulets from streets or hills collect in a valley, they will form a current of increased volume and force, that will still bear onward its accumulation of sediment.

If, now, the stream enter a pond or lake the current will widen, and so lose its force, and this heterogeneous mass of material, will be assorted and distributed somewhat as follows. The heavier particles, that is, the gravel, will sink first and be deposited in a bed of comparatively narrow limits near the entrance of the stream. The sand, being lighter, will be borne farther out, till the current can carry it no longer, when it will sink, and in consequence be distributed over a wider surface and above the gravel. And if the quantity of sand and gravel be about equal, it is evident the layer of sand will be as much thinner than that of the gravel, as the area covered is greater.

Sediment gathered and distributed.

Then, again, the silt—finely comminuted clay, called dust when dry—being still lighter than sand, will be borne still farther out, and distributed in consequence over a still larger area than either of the others.

And, now, when in process of ages these beds of sedimentary deposits solidify—change to solid rock, the lower bed will be conglomerate, the middle one sandstone, and the upper slate. A similar process goes on, on a much larger scale in the ocean, especially in the formation of the two varieties last named, but the smaller body of water is more convenient for our purpose of illustration.

But there is another important matter to be considered in this connection.

In case of heavy rains various fragments of organic remains, vegetable or animal, are likely to be washed into the stream and deposited with the other sediment. Such a fragment may be buried in the gravel, in the sand, or in the silt; and so imbedded becomes a fossil, that may appear if the ledge of rock is ever opened. It is clear that it must drift in and be deposited while the sediment is gathering and before it is solidified. And we may, therefore, conclude that such fossil is a relic of a plant or animal that lived on the earth when that rock was forming, or at no very long period before; and that it, therefore, gives us a clue to the kind of life in that period. *Origin of fossils.*

The chances of the fossil being preserved, however, depend largely on the particular bed into which it falls. *Preservation of fossils.*

Conglomerate is not favorable for the preservation of a foreign body: first, because the gravel tends to grind and destroy it; and, second, because the rock being porous, water percolates through and tends to dissolve it. Nor is the slate much more favorable. Owing to the crystallizing process that makes the slate bed easily divisible into thin plates, the form of the fossil is likely to be distorted beyond recognition, if not entirely destroyed. Of the formations described, therefore, the sandstone is likely to show most fossils in a fair state of preservation. We have now indicated the mode of origin of three important kinds of rocks. There is a fourth, formed in a different way, we must also notice, as it is the most important of all the fossilliferous series.

Lime, which makes up so large a portion of the rock systems, is held in solution in the waters of the sea as well as of lakes and rivers, and contributes largely to the structure of both animals and plants. When an animal dies, its skeleton, whether bone or shell, is readily transformed into limestone, unless the conditions are entirely adverse. And many limestone beds are made up almost wholly of such remains. From the earliest formation of sedimentary rocks, this process has been going on, especially in the sea, and is still going on.

Origin of limestone.

With each geological epoch, a new layer of limestone is added to some part of the earth's crust.

Oftentimes these remains lose their shape entirely, may be finely powdered by a process of attrition, or crushed and folded by superincumbent pressure, before the bed is finally solidified. Or, after solidification they may undergo a sort of metamorphosis by which the original structure is lost, though the substance remains, as in finely grained marble which is nothing but common limestone changed by pressure and heat.

And, again, the fossils may be unearthed ages on ages after they are deposited, almost as distinctly shaped as they were in life. They contribute in either case, however, to the substance of the bed of which they form a part.

With this analysis of rock formations, if we will briefly recall the divisions and distinctions before noted in the animal and vegetable kingdoms, whence all fossils come, we shall now be able to make out a fairly complete history of life on the earth, from its early if not its first appearance, to the present era.

Plants are divisible into three general classes, distinguished by their modes of growth and fruiting or seeding, and conveniently designated as Acrogens, Endogens, and Exogens. We need not restate the distinctions in detail. *The vegetable kingdom.*

The animal kingdom is divisible into five general classes: Protozoans, Radiates, Mollusks, Articulates, and Vertebrates, the distinc *The animal kingdom.*

tions between which will be readily recalled. The first is represented by the infusoria and the sponge; the second by the coral and the star-fish; the third by the snail on land and oyster in the sea; the fourth by the worm on land, the insect in the air, and lobster in the sea; and the fifth by the fish, reptile, bird, quadruped, and man.

We have, then, before us a view of the principal rock formations in which fossils may be found. And also the two sources or kingdoms which contribute fossils to the rocks when forming.

And, now, to the record itself.

<small>Origin of earliest rocks.</small> The first formed rocks were, of course, of igneous origin—came out of the fire, or were solidified by cooling from a molten state. In these there could have been no life or remains of life; for till after this period, no living thing could have existed on the earth, by reason of the intense heat. Moreover, the first formed rocks, resulting from the cooling process, must have been corroded on the surface and worn away, forming soft beds of soil, either on the rocks, or by drifting, at the bottom of the sea, before there could have been any kind of even vegetable life. But this seems not to have been long delayed, for in very early beds of sedimentary rocks are found traces of some forms of life.

For convenience we adopt the geologist's designations of the successive eras or ages. [*See chart following this lecture.*]

The earliest *sedimentary* rocks of any considerable extent are known as the Laurentian, and in parts of America are estimated to have attained a thickness or depth of thirty thousand feet. The period in which they were formed was long supposed to have been lifeless. But recent discoveries have changed that conclusion. The plants, as plants, have entirely disappeared, no form of one being distinguishable in fossil.   *Earliest sedimentary rocks.*

But the existence of extensive beds of graphite —sometimes, though incorrectly, styled black lead—in the Laurentian rocks, implies the existence of plants in that period. For since graphite is believed to have the same origin as coal, namely from plants, it could not have been formed before there were plants of which to form it.   *Earliest evidence of life (Graphite).*

And as the first distinguishable plants above this formation are all of the first and simplest class, namely Acrogens, we have the best of reasons for presuming the Laurentian plants, or the plants which grew when the Laurentian rocks were forming, were entirely of this class.

Moreover, some diligent explorers, notably Dr. J. W. Dawson, of McGill College, Montreal, has discovered in the upper or later Laurentian, the fossil of an animal, Eozoon (dawning life), so simple and yet so obscure in structure, that its organic character is still in some doubt. If it is an animal, as it probably is, it is of the very lowest form, one of the minor Protozoans. Life began at the lowest point, and with the simplest mode of growth. Here, then, we find the introduction of life upon the earth, in the form of plants, and possibly of animals also. The occurrence of limestone and beds of iron ore in the same formation are also regarded as *signs* of the existence of some kind of life, since these owe their origin chiefly to organic agency. But little account has yet been made of this fact by the geologist, however, in dealing with the Laurentian rocks.

<small>The Eozoon.</small>

We now move up one step in the series.

Next in order after the Laurentian came the Silurian rocks, so named from a district in England where they show at the surface. They are made up of successive series of beds of sandstone, limestone, and shale (a soft irregular slate), nature having now got fairly to work, wearing away rocks, transporting the abraded material by means of wind and ocean currents, and building them up in other places.

<small>The Silurian formation.</small>

We find in these rocks the remains of both

plants and animals, many still of low type and very simple structure, such as the sea-weed among plants and the sponge and coral among animals; but there are found also both plants and animals of higher forms and more varied constitutions, showing a great advance over the life of the former period.

The Radiates doubtless existed in great numbers, especially corals and crinoids, or flower animals, as they are sometimes called by reason of their peculiar shape; but as they are fragile or pulpy in substance, and therefore easily destroyed, they do not appear in great numbers in the rocks. But the Mollusk, with his strong shell to protect him in life and keep his memory alive when he is dead, appeared in strong force, and some beds of the Silurian rocks, as those which appear at Trenton Falls, New York, are composed almost wholly of its remains. To walk along the shelving banks of that stream (Canada Creek), or on portions of its dry bed when the water is low, as it is sometimes late in summer, is to tread upon millions of skeletons or casements of these animals that lived in the sea in the Silurian age.

This formation, extending eastward into Vermont, was metamorphosed or crystallized in the upheaval of the Green Mountains, and constitutes the extensive marble beds of that region. *The Green Mountain marble.*

.There was as yet little if any life upon the land. The ocean was inhabited—the scene, perhaps, of strife and depredation; the land was almost utterly bare and still.

The plants of this period either did not advance so rapidly, or, as seems more proba-
Plants of the Silurian age. ble, their softer substance rendered them more liable to destruction in the geologic convulsions and revolutions that marked, at that early day, the changes from one period to another. What plants do reveal themselves, however, show a considerable variety, including a large number of marine plants and in the upper layers a few that grew on the land. Some additions have been made by recent explorations, and others may still be added to the list. The whole number of plants that can be identified is small in comparison with the number of animals, and they are chiefly if not entirely of the class of Acrogens. This difference in number is nothing remarkable, however, considering the readiness with which tender herbage yields to the action of the elements.

Leaving now the Silurian we pass next to the
The Devonian formation. Devonian formation, named also from an English district. Hugh Miller styled it the "Old Red Sandstone." And here we shall find some marked changes in the types of life among both animals and plants. First the

plants were much more numerous; or if not more numerous in growth, then more successfully preserved in fossil. They belong chiefly still to the first class of plants, though one or two, of higher but uncertain type, have been identified. It must be borne in mind that the extent of sea was much greater than at a later period, and that of land correspondingly less. And this may account for the fact that the plants continued of that class that flourishes best in the sea, or in immediate proximity to it. The higher plants require high and comparatively dry land.

But the animal life of the Devonian period was abundant and varied. Not only did the Mollusks hold a place, as to numbers, almost equalling that of their Silurian congeners, differing merely in slight structural details, attaining perhaps something more of symmetry and something more of distinctive character; and the Radiates, especially corals, multiply and extend with great rapidity and contribute their short-lived skeletons to the forming rocks, and the Articulate—insect—begin to wing its way upon the humid air, but the fish also appeared, which, having a backbone, belongs to the highest class of animals, the Vertebrates.

The latter were of considerable variety and vast numbers, insomuch that the period is known in geology as the Age of Fishes. It was evidently also a time of depredation and reprisals among these denizens of the deep. And many of them were amply equipped for the fray. They had coats of mail, consisting of thick bony plates, with carapace, like a shield about the head, and sharp spike-like teeth that not only fitted them for self-defence, but must have made them the terror of their less securely armored neighbors. But such is the way of animal life. The stronger subsist upon the weaker. And but for their prodigious rapidity of increase, " bringing forth abundantly," the tribes of smaller animals would long ago have disappeared. What is lost in one way, however, is gained in another, and nature is never defeated of her ends by any casual contingency.

Age of Fishes.

We move now one step farther upward in the scale.

Next in order above the Devonian rocks comes the Carboniferous system, including the extensive coal formations which supply so important a necessity to-day. In this period the development of plants was most remarkable, both as to numbers and variety. Hitherto we have found very few higher than the first and lowest class. In the coal period this division still held the leading place. They grew to enormous size, and formed rank and tangled

The coal period.

jungles in the low and marshy districts which bordered on the sea, and held some low valleys of the interior.

The tree-fern, the sigillaria a huge club-moss, and the calamite a giant rush, were among the striking forms of vegetable life. To these were due the vast accumulations of vegetable matter of which the coal beds were formed. Crushed down and pressed together beneath still later rock formations, they lost their fibrous structure and were thus metamorphosed into the coal that serves the world so well.

But though Acrogens still held the first rank in point of numbers and probably of size, they did not comprise the entire vegetation of the period. The higher types, introduced sparingly in the preceding period, now advanced to a place of some importance. Exogens appeared upon the uplands and drifted, sometimes in the form of prostrate trunks, into the swamps, where the coal plants proper grew. The varieties of Exogens were few, however, and bore a remote resemblance to some of the pines of the modern world. *Variety of plants.*

The period was remarkable for this fact, that it first comprehended all the general classes of vegetable life. What changes followed in succeeding ages consisted in new orders and varieties, not new modes of growth. The system of plant life was complete.

The same remark will apply to the animal kingdom in the period of the coal formations.

The Protozoans still existed as they had from the early dawn of life. Among Radiates the corals were less luxuriant than in the preceding age, for much of the shallow sea had a muddy bottom, which corals do not like.

<small>Variety of animals.</small>

The Mollusks still held important rank, and left their contributions of shells to the forming rocks.

The Articulates grew into more importance, and included a few related to the trilobite, that luxuriated in the mud along the borders of the seas and lakes, and insects that crawled in and out among the reeking plants, or buzzed and hummed in myriad numbers in the moist warm atmosphere. While among Vertebrates, the fishes of the Devonian period were greatly reduced in numbers and in part superseded by different species; and several varieties of creatures classed among the reptiles were added, especially those of amphibious nature. The system of life was thus complete, both in the animal and the vegetable kingdoms. There were no new general classes or divisions to be added, though the variety of orders, families, and species that followed was almost numberless.

And now there came a change in the method of advance; beginning with forms of extraordinary size, first plants and then animals — the natural order, observe — and then subordinating size to other and higher characteristics. *Change in method of advance.*

This series of changes began in the coal period, when plants attained to gigantic proportions, and was followed, as we shall find by taking another upward step, by the Reptilian Age, during the formation of the Mesozoic (middle life) rocks. *Age of Reptiles.*

In this period all the several classes of animals existed, in more or less numerous types, from the Protozoan to the Vertebrate, and the usual processes of rock formation went on; but the reptile, introduced sparingly, in the form of a few swimming lizards and the like, in the preceding age, now assumed the leading place in the animal creation, and gave name to the age as known in geological history.

Among the reptiles of the period were the following:

The Plesiosaurus, a swimming saurian, with snake-like neck sometimes of forty vertebræ, a small head, with slender teeth, a body compact and flexible, and provided with small paddles for pushing its way through the water; the Ichthyosaurus (fish-lizard) unlike the foregoing in almost every particular, sometimes thirty feet in length, with jaws six feet long, set with sabre-like teeth, and eyes of enormous size; the Mosasaurus, the sea-serpent of the period, as Dana aptly describes it, seventy-five feet in length and provided with double rows of saw-like teeth for seizing its prey and tearing it; the Pterosaurians (flying reptiles) loathsome creatures bearing some resemblance to the modern bat; the Labyrinthodont, with the habits of the frog, but as large almost as a common ox; and the immense creatures, whether bird or biped reptile, is yet uncertain, that left their footprints in great numbers in the red sandstone of the Connecticut valley.

Prof. O. C. Marsh, of Yale College, has also, by his untiring industry and enterprise, added largely to the list of reptiles from the Mesozoic rocks in the Rocky Mountain region.

Prof. O. C. Marsh's discoveries.

Chief among these are the Holosaurus, similar to the Ichthyosaurus, but more serpent-like, and sometimes seventy-five feet in length; the Atlantosaurus, crocodilian in type, but immensely larger than the modern alligator; and a bird he names the Hesperornis "essentially a carnivorous swimming ostrich," which had teeth, and stood full six feet high.

There were also great plants in this age, as there were in the age preceding; with an advance in number of those belonging to the highest class, including the sassafras, hickory, willow beech, and poplar. But the reptiles furnished the striking and characteristic feature of the period. It was the Age of Reptiles.

The next upward step brings us to the Cenozoic (recent life), better known as the Tertiary period, and distinguished also as the Age of Mammals. The name "Tertiary" is retained from the early nomenclature, when the terms *primary* and *secondary* were applied to the preceding rock-formations. It has no special appropriateness now, but is retained for old acquaintance sake.

<small>The Tertiary formation (Age of Mammals).</small>

But the designation, "Age of Mammals," is specially appropriate. The mammals, among animals, held the leading place. The reptiles, remanded to a subordinate position, declined in size and numbers. Among fishes, those with skeletons of bone instead of cartilage (introduced in the preceding age) had become most numerous, and there was a general approach in the animal kingdom toward modern types.

The mammals were of large size, but otherwise, in many points like those that live to-day. Among those characteristic of the period were the Mammoth, a gigantic elephant, and the Mastodon, the Zeuglodon, bearing some resemblance to the whale but with great molar-teeth, and the Dinoceras, a huge creature, larger than the rhinoceros, and very similar in habit.

Prof. Marsh has laid the scientific world under further obligations by additions to this list taken from the tertiary formations of the "Terres mauvaises" (bad lands) in our western territories. The list includes the Orohippus, Miohippus, and their congeners, in which Prof. Huxley so confidently traces the lineage of the horse.

<small>Recent additions from our western territories.</small>

The plants of the Tertiary, included all the general classes, but the larger proportion were of the second and third, or the middle and highest divisions, and approached in form and variety those of the present time. Many of these, also, were of extraordinary size. A fragment of a palm-leaf found in the upper Missouri region, must have measured when complete, twelve feet in length, and there were trees closely related to the giant Sequoias, "big trees," of California. The life of the period was by no means usurped, however, by plants or animals of great size.

<small>Great plants of the Tertiary.</small>

There are, both in Europe and America, extensive deposits in the rocks of the period, made up almost wholly of siliceous shells, so minute, it is computed by Ehrenberg, that a cubic inch contains more than forty thousand millions. Infusorial earth. And the nummulitic limestones of Southern Europe and Northern Africa, the same of which some of the Egyptian pyramids are built, are made up chiefly of the shells of very minute animals. The forms of life were even more numerous than they had been before, and the most insignificant among them seems to have filled some important place in the economy of the world.

And, now, one more upward step in the rock formations and we come to the Age of Man, of which there is no need that we speak in much detail. The period is passing now. Quaternary Age (Age of Man). Intelligence and moral power, other than those concerned in the creation from the first, are become potent factors in the life upon the earth; and all the ambitions and hopes of men find fields of exercise in the tasks it sets before them, and the rewards it holds out to them.

[*The Quaternary Age will be discussed in Lecture XI.*]

Our life history of the earth is now complete.

We began with its early dawning. We found the evidence of plants remaining in the graphite mines, where the plants themselves had disappeared. We found next the Review.

simplest class of plants in fossil. Next came a few, sparingly distributed, which rank in the higher class, herbs bearing seed; and lastly, growing side by side with these, the fruit and nut-growing trees.

We turned, then, to the animal kingdom. Contemporaneous with these varieties of plants we found the various classes of the animal world. The Protozoan first; a mere "moving thing," almost destitute of organism, but followed in an upward scale by the Radiate (coral), the Mollusk (shell-fish), the Articulate (insect), and the Vertebrate, beginning with the fishes and advancing to the reptile, bird, quadruped, and man. Our task is done. We have read the record in the rocks.

We have made no attempt, it will be observed, to estimate the age of the earth, or to calculate that of any single layer of the rocks. It cannot be done, except approximately, and then with much uncertainty.

<small>Age of the earth.</small>

It is computed it may require a thousand years, under ordinary circumstances, to form a bed of limestone one foot in depth, and possibly five to ten thousand years to form one foot of coal.

Lyell estimates the accumulations of the Mississippi delta at about nineteen inches in a century, and that of the Nile mud at less than four inches. Dana computes the most rapid growth of coral reefs at one sixteenth of an inch per annum, and Le Conte estimates it at one to two feet in a century. But all such data are illusive.

Two beds of rock forming side by side may differ in their rates of growth, and the same bed may vary from year to year, or century to century. It depends on the material at command, and on the regularity of the currents by which it is deposited. It is comparatively easy to decide which strata are the oldest, by their position or by the fossils they contain. But we know nothing definite of the time required to form them, nor of the time that has elapsed since they were compacted.

There are other means of estimating the age of the earth, as a whole, as by its temperature and the erosive action of water, and yet the best authorities differ widely on the subject.

A distinguished astronomer estimates the age of the earth since a crust first formed upon it at fifty-seven million years. Sir William Thompson calculates it at one hundred million years. The evolutionists demand more time. They say, whatever may be the necessities of rock formations, that a hundred million years is not sufficient for the Ascidian to develop into a man. We suspect they are correct. But Prof. Proctor would seem to satisfy all reasonable demands in this direction, when he places the age of the earth at four hundred and fifty million years. But we have said enough to indicate the uncertain character of all such calculations. We can reach but one sure and safe conclusion; that if we estimate the time in years, the earth is very old.

GEOLOGICAL CHART.

Eras.	Ages.		Characteristic Life.
CENOZOIC.	Quaternary Age, or Age of Man.	Periods or Epochs of the Quaternary.	Present. Terrace. Champlain. Glacial.
	Tertiary Age, or Age of Mammals.		Palm, Magnolia, Myrtle, Fig, Beech, Poplar, Maple, Oak. Infusoria, Oyster, Fishes, Peccary, Mastodon, Rhinoceros, Orohippus, Miohippus.
MESOZOIC.	Mesozoic Age, or Age of Reptiles.		Cycads, Conifers, Plane-tree, Willow, Sassafras, Holly, Redwood, Cypress. Plesiosauras, Ichthyosaurus, Pterodactyl, Labyrinthodont, Atlantosaurus, Ammonite, Hesperornis.
PALEOZOIC	Carboniferous Age, or Age of Coal Plants.		Tree-ferns, Sigillaria, Lepidodendron, Calamite, Conifers. Rhizopods, Corals, Crinoids, Snails, Insects, Lizards, Amphibians.
	Devonian Age, or Age of Fishes.		Ferns, Lycopods, Conifers. Corals, Spirifer, Nautilus, Trilobite, FISHES (Ganoids and Sharks).
	Silurian Age, or Age of Mollusks.		Sea-Weeds (Fucoids). Sponge, Coral, Crinoid, Trilobite, MOLLUSKS, in great variety.
EOZOIC.	Laurentian Age.		Sea-Weeds. Eozoon.

Igneous Rocks—Lifeless Period.

VII.

Man.

"God created man in his own image."

       " Still I own
A love that spreads from zone to zone;
No time the sacred fire can smother!
Where breathes the man, I hail the brother.
Man! how sublime—from heaven his birth—
The God's bright image walks the earth!
And if, at times, his footstep strays,
I pity where I may not praise."

VII.

ORIGIN OF MAN AND UNITY OF THE RACE.

A GENIAL writer of our own time has said: "Once the great question with men was, Where are we all going to? Now the question that commands chief attention is, Where did we all come from?" And in the present state of the public mind it is hardly possible to allude to the history of man or his relations to the world, but that this question will come to the front. *[side note: The question of Origin.]*

The old familiar theory is that man was a direct and immediate creation of God. Another theory is that he has *developed*, by a process called *Evolution*, out of the lower orders of the animal kingdom. The latter theory assumes different forms, but the one best known, perhaps, is that coupled with the name of Charles Darwin, and known as "Evolution by Natural Selection."

There is, first, a difference of opinion among

evolutionists themselves as to the primal origin of life; some assuming that life is a product of matter in certain conditions, and others that at some remote period in the earth's history germs of life were introduced, out of which all the forms of life have grown. Without attempting to settle definitely the question of primal origin, Mr. Darwin's theory, as we read it, is this—that after life was *started* on the earth, there were sufficient causes in nature to bring out of the first germs all the varieties that have since existed. As a single illustration of the principle involved, it is said, that the flipper of the whale, the wing of the bird, the fore-leg of the quadruped, and the arm of man are essentially the same in structure; and each in turn developed out of the next lower and preceding type, and that similar analogies may be traced in other parts of the body; that *function* determines *form*, and that the use a member of the body serves determines the shape it takes.

Doctrine of Evolution.

There is no time now to trace the evidence in detail for or against this theory. But after a somewhat careful consideration of the subject, and much that has been said and written upon it, we are constrained to say that so far as revealing any connection between man and the brutes, the doctrine of evolution fails utterly.

Our reasons for such decided statement are these:—

Mr. Darwin's theory proceeds on the assumption that "nature makes no leaps;" that the change from one animal or race to its *immediate* follower must be very slight. And, therefore, that if two animals differ in any considerable degree, it is certain that the one did not proceed directly from the other, but that there were intermediate links, even though we do not find those links and cannot *prove* that such ever existed. {Postulate of Darwinism.}

Now the nearest approach to man is in that type of the monkey tribe known as the Ape. Mr. Huxley, in a little book entitled "Man's Place in Nature," has very carefully traced out certain striking resemblances between the ape and man. And Prof. Mivart has ably supplemented him in his "Man and Apes." The brain of the largest anthropoid ape is smaller, the chest larger, the lower limbs shorter, the upper limbs much longer than in man. The ape can walk on two feet like man, though he generally goes on four. He can stand quite erect, though more inclined to a stooping posture. But while it is possible for the ape thus to stand and walk, the arrangement of the bones and position of the brain plainly indicate that his natural position is {Man and the Ape.}

on four feet rather than on two. Such are some of the considerations on which the argument for a genetic connection between man and the ape are based.

But the theory that there has been a series of advances from the lowest animals, through the monkey tribe, culminating in man, is involved in grave perplexities, unless we suppose some characteristic of the animal, though lost to its immediate offspring, may be recovered by a remoter generation. The highest tribes of monkies do not show the closest resemblance to man. The gorilla is accounted the highest, or possibly the chimpanzee may have equal rank. The baboon and gibbon stand lower, and the spider monkey lowest of all the old world tribes. But in point of anatomical structure, the lower approach man more nearly than those that hold the highest rank. For instance, man has twelve pairs of ribs and five lumbar vertebræ. The gorilla has thirteen pairs of ribs and three or four vertebræ, while some of the lower apes have the same number, both of ribs and vertebræ as man. Long hair on the head and face, resembling that of man, is found in some of the lower apes; never in the highest. In the arrangement and structure of the teeth, the half-apes resemble man more nearly than the highest species. The ape having the frontal shape of the skull most like man ranks fourth in the scale below the gorilla or chimpanzee. In fact there is no regularly ascending series culminating in man, or distinctly pointing to him.

Mr. Darwin admits this anomaly, and calls it *Reversion*, on the same principle, as we interpret him, that a child may have the black eyes of its grandfather though its father's eyes are blue and its mother's gray; and that it may show some other resemblance to ancestors still more remote. But this theory as applied to anatomical structure, is a direct contradiction of the principle on which he lays so much stress, that evolution by natural selection requires a constant advance. *The doctrine of Reversion.*

Moreover, naturalists tell us that in all the higher groups of animals their relative rank is determined by the brain. Now we have the best authority for saying that the largest ape's brain measures not more than thirty-four and a half inches, while the smallest brain of man—with *very* rare exceptions—measures sixty-three inches; that of man being nearly double that of the ape. And this is the proportion Mr. Huxley adopts in his comparison. *Brain of man and ape.*

There is no animal that comes between these two; and so far as we can ascertain there never was an animal whose rank would place it between them. There is no connecting link living—no trace of any in the recent rocks. And now, recalling the postulate on which Mr. Darwin's theory proceeds, that if animals differ in any considerable degree it is certain that one did not proceed directly from the other, but that there were several links between —here are two animals differing by one half in the size of the brain. It is not possible for nature to make such a leap, and the one could not, therefore, have sprung directly from the other. If there is any connection between them it must be through intermediate links. But there are no intermediate links, and no evidence that such links ever existed.

Prof. Asa Gray suggests that man did not descend from the monkey, but that the line of development branched farther back.

Prof. Gray's suggestion.

But this only makes the possibility of tracing man's lineage the more hopeless.

This, then, is the ground of the statement that so far as man is concerned, the doctrine of evolution by natural selection, or by the operation of merely natural causes, fails utterly and absolutely.

We are aware that some attempt is made to explain the absence of these supposed intermediate types:

The "Missing Links."

I. It is said that their remains may have perished with the lapse of ages. That might be possible, if the monkey had existed in very remote times. But, on the contrary, it is quite a recent animal; the earliest fossils not dating back beyond the Cenozoic, or recent rocks.

II. It is said, again, that some great convulsion of nature, even in recent times, may have destroyed all or most of the animals existing at the time, and these intermediate types may have been among them. But there are the most abundant fossils of other animals covering the whole of the recent period; so that if higher tribes of monkeys or lower tribes of men had existed, it is hardly possible that all trace of them could have disappeared.

III. Another curious and certainly very slender assumption is based on the fact that casual mention is made by some ancient authors, of an island called Atlantis; and, since no such island is known to-day, it is gravely assumed that it has disappeared in the sea, and that it *may* have carried down the missing links.

In reply, it may be said:

1. There is no sufficient evidence that there ever was such an island as Atlantis. There is no mention of it in authentic history, and the occasional allusions and traditions do not agree as to its locality.

<small>The myth Atlantis.</small>

2. If there ever was such an island, it is by no means certain that it has disappeared, for it may

be known to-day by some other name; as the island of Corfu is the Corcyra of two or three thousand years ago, and the ancient names of some places have been lost beyond recovery.

3. Suppose there was such an island, and that in some great convulsion it did disappear beneath the waves, there is still not one shred of proof that it carried down man or monkey, or anything even remotely allied to either of them.

And still, on such precarious threads will men hang sober arguments to bolster a doubtful cause or defend a favorite theory. And Prof. Hæckel, the most daring and least reliable of all the prominent evolutionists, expresses his philosophical dismay, not to say his natural disgust, that intelligent men of science will longer doubt the doctrine of evolution.

If, then, man was not developed by natural causes out of the inferior animals, whence came he?

Here we find ourselves compelled to fall back on that very ancient document, the opening of the book of Genesis, not because it is the only evidence we have, but because we find the matter nowhere else so clearly and so concisely stated.

The Hebrew record. "And God said, let us make man in our own image; and let them have dominion over the fish of the sea, and over the fowl of the air, and over the cattle and over all the earth. So God created man in His own image." Of man's mastery in the earth and over it, we can ourselves bear witness, for that mastery he still retains. And after all that has been said and written, it must be confessed this is the only theory of the origin of man that after each assault and partial surrender but roots itself the deeper in the minds and hearts of men.

It is worthy of remark that the word "create," used in the beginning with reference to the world as a whole, is used here with reference to man, and that it occurs but once between, and then, as it seems, incidentally. Whether we are to understand by this, that the creation of man was more a direct operation of the divine power than the creation of other animals and of the plants, or whether it is merely a recurrence of the word to avoid repetition of another, we do not attempt to decide.

But certain it is that in the beginning the world is said to have been due to the *immediate act of the Creator*, nothing else intervening. So here it is said God *created* man. It was thus the act of God, and the culmination of His plan in the world.

But right here we encounter another perplexing problem. It relates to the different races of man. Did they have a common origin? Our answer must be brief. *The question of race.*

In the first place, all men, whatever their land

or origin, have almost the same anatomical structure, with similar habits both of body and mind. They are subject to the same diseases. They live, under like conditions, about the same length of time. They all shape implements and make use of fire. They all believe in God; all resort to prayer; all have funeral ceremonies over their dead, and all believe in a future life. There are individual exceptions, but this is the rule. And that they are all of one *species* is evident from the fact that any two races may intermarry, and the increase will go on as if each race was confined wholly to itself.

But there are a variety of races differing in color and to some extent in physiognomy. Whence came these differences? As they are found divided as to geographical locality, it has been suggested, that they originated in different sections of the world, and sprang from different progenitors. But before we make any such assumption it is well to consider whether climate and habits of life may not in process of time, produce these differences, though all were of the same family to begin with.

1. As to geography and clime. In northern Europe the characteristic complexion is light, and the hair is light and straight: witness the Swedes. In southern Europe, the characteristic complexion is dark, and the hair black with a tendency to curl: witness the French

Climatic variations.

and Italians. In the interior of Europe, as in Germany, these characteristics are not so marked either way. In other words, they are between the two extremes, as the locality is between the two first-named. Then cross to Arabia and Egypt, and we find the complexion still more dark and the countenance still more widely different from those of the north. And yet there is no doubt that these all belong to the same race. The Swede, the Frenchman, and the Arab all belong to the *Caucasian* race. If we go into the interior of Africa we shall find people with black skin and woolly hair. But on the coast of Mozambique are people about as dark skinned as Africans, with features more like the Arab, while on their heads they have a crisply curled or frizzled hair, something between the curly hair of southern Europe and the wool of Africa.

2. Then take a single illustration that can be traced somewhat easily. There is no people of more marked physiognomical expression than the Jews—dark complexion, round face, and black hair. Moreover, as they rarely intermarry with other people, these features are remarkably well preserved. And yet in some of the bitter persecutions that befel the Jews centuries ago, some of them took refuge in Northern Russia; and though they are not believed to have intermarried with others, but

to be still pure-blooded Jews, there are some among them now with red hair and blue eyes. Such changes are wrought, in the course of a few generations, by climate and condition. And it is evident that the variations might be greater still, if the time was longer and the change of climate and condition yet more radical.

So, notwithstanding all the speculations on the subject, it must be said in all candor, there is no sufficient proof, as yet, that there was more than one primal pair; but that all men are of one family and one blood.

But even if it should be proved that there were more than one primal pair, it does not invalidate the account given in Genesis, for since human nature is everywhere essentially the same, the record of the one pair would serve as an example for the whole. We should then say that Adam and Eve were the *historic* pair; the ones chosen as representatives of the whole.*

The historic race.

What, then, of the constitution of man? "So God created man in his own image." No one

---

* As these pages go to press a volume by Dr. Alexander Winchell appears, entitled "PRE-ADAMITES," in which the author assumes, what others had before suggested, that Adam was the progenitor only of the white race. On the other hand, Dr. E. B. Tylor, of London, a very high authority, says recent evidences greatly strengthen the probability that all men are of one original stock.

probably supposes the likeness here to be in physical form or appearance, or if in that, not in that alone.

In bodily constitution, man is an animal. He is made up of organs and parts having each a specific function. He is flesh and bone and blood; fed with nutritious food, baned with poisons—suffering from neglect, from disease or accident, and returning to the dust when the life is gone out of him. So far he is an animal. *Man an animal.*

But this is not all of him; this is not what makes him a man as distinguished from an animal. He has spiritual faculties, as well as animal powers; and in *this* is he created in the divine similitude. He has intellectual faculties of such breadth and strength that no one has ever dared to say what achievements he might attain; for in the narrow span of human life there is not time to get these powers fairly into working order. He has sentiments and impulses out of which grow the humanest sympathies and the sweetest charities; and aspirations that lead him to holiness of life and to supreme trust in the power above that is more than life. All the heroes and the martyrs that glorify the pages of history go to tell us there is something more in man than that which grows out of fleshly tissue and bony structure. Admit that there are bold contrasts and sharp distinctions among men; one man base almost to the level of brutality, and another self-sacrificing and devoted as man can be, the contrast only shows the more clearly, the difference between that which is merely brutish and that which constitutes the man. So let us understand what man is in his natural constitution. Then we can trace his history. One broad distinction between man and the inferior animal is that the latter is controlled by instincts; the former is the subject of his own intelligence. We do not mean that man has no instincts, for he has; or that the animal shows no trace of reason, for he does. But that the practical limit of reason is soon reached in the animal, and then in emergency he falls back on his instinct, while in man instinct is soon outgrown by the exercise of reason, and to that exercise no limit in all experience has ever been approached. So marked is this difference between the animal and man, that we do not hesitate to condemn in the one what we praise without stint in the other. The dog droops and dies on the grave of his dead master, and we admire his fidelity; but it would be an ignoble thing for a man to do. When Hamlet in the play leaps into the grave of Ophelia, if he were a dog he would crouch and perish there. But because he is not a dog, but a *living soul*—with hopes and faith and aspirations, he rouses himself from his deep despondency, and comes forth to battle yet farther with the stern realities of an already overshadowed life. In the fact that man was created in the image of God we find the explanation, then, of the various powers and faculties that exalt him above the animal.

What, finally, of his history?

The same record that tells us he was given dominion over the earth, gives us farther on a picture of his life in a "garden," or in "a land of loveliness," as some authors render it, wherein, to the outward seeming, was everything necessary for the sustenance and prosperity of human life. But a strange blight soon came over this auspicious opening, for these favored subjects disobeyed the law of God and fell; and thence came pains and penalties they had never known before. *[History of man.]*

And, now, how came this strange event about?

There is nothing more natural in the experience of the human race. It was the beginning of that long conflict which is as old as human nature, and destined possibly to continue as long as man dwells upon the earth —"the conflict of duty with desire." *[Duty vs. desire.]*

Desire is here presented in the figure of the serpent. The serpent has no power of speech or other means of communicating thought to man—

if thought it ever had. But nothing is so suggestive of the serpent that comes upon us unawares, as that subtle something we call temptation, which is rooted in the very nature of every moral being, or every being that takes account of right and wrong. And it was because human nature was so constituted, that the conflict began in Eden with such consequences as are written in the biblical account. Eden was a state of *innocence*. That is what especially distinguishes it in our minds to-day. It was a state of *ignorance* as well. This is a point we are apt to overlook; that human education as yet was scarce begun. There was no history, there was no observation, there was no experience of human life; none of the agencies by which men grow and learn. There is danger that in our contemplation of this subject we shall forget one of these potent facts, in our admiration for the other.

They were created in innocence and in ignorance; innocent as the little child, which is unconscious of immodesty or any sense of shame, though utterly unclad; ignorant of any such thing as good and evil, or that there was any difference between them. So much the record implies, in the very plainest terms. But in them was born a disposition to inquire and learn; a spirit of curiosity, if you choose to call it so:

<small>Primal condition of man.</small>

an inclination to pry into the hidden things about them.

Put your child, who has not yet learned to stand in awe of you, into a room in which is everything that can amuse and entertain, and say to him, "You may have free range here, *except in that drawer;* there is something you must not see." That is the very first place he will go to. That is human nature. And it is not a vicious disposition. It is the spirit of inquiry and discovery, which, to whatever strange excesses and sad results it may lead us sometimes, is the key to all progress.

The first pair in Eden were warned before the act, it is said, but there is nothing that teaches like experience. And in the absence of any chance to observe effects in others, a warning is but a theory that lacks confirmation. The little child attracted by the burning taper, tries to seize it with his hand. The mother warns him a hundred times, and still he does not understand what harm there can be in it. Let him get his hand into the blaze but once, and it satisfies him for a lifetime.

In this we have an example in different form of the experience that came to man in paradise, and has been a regular inheritance of each generation and of every human being from then till now; and what did the first pair learn from this experience?

Results of experience.

1. That there was a Power above them to which they were in subjection.
2. That there was such a thing in human life as duty, and obligation, and responsibility.

But that which most forcibly impressed itself upon them, and that is magnified in the account, was that there was a penalty attached to disobedience. And they learned at once, therefore, the advantage of a strict observance of the divine law in relation to human life. And thus it was that, from their first estate of ignorance, their "eyes were opened," and they knew good and evil—though from their estate of innocence they fell.

Man was turned out of Eden, it is said. And who, from his childish innocence has come to be conscious of base desires and evil purposes, has not realized something very like this in his own experience? Who that goes on in evil ways does not sometimes feel himself estranged from God and all pure and holy things, while his own conscience is the watchful guardian, with flaming sword, that keeps the gate. Adam was not to be an idle spectator of the world; his task was set "to dress and keep the garden" when he was first placed therein. And so to work is the mission of man on the earth, and always was. And while this, in obedience to intelligence and law, may be only a delight, we know full well how indolence and vice and crime multiply the hardships and penalties of life. Adam was the first to pass through this experience, and so he stands for the human race throughout the Bible record; but he was not the last.

Every child born into this world repeats, with more or less completeness, the experience of this far-off progenitor. He has his little experience of Eden to begin with, when in unconscious innocence he knows nothing of evil or of good; nothing of duty, responsibility, or obligation. He soon passes that, for he has an inheritance of evil tendencies, whatever may have been the fact at first. Human experience repeated.

He soon passes the early stage, we repeat—"dies to innocence." And the long and old-time conflict between duty and desire begins, with such variety of results as we witness in human life.

And is every human life a failure, then? Nay, not so. There was an Eden back of us; there is a paradise beyond. The first was given us as our inheritance; the other we must win. The penalty that followed the first disobedience was offset in some degree by the knowledge that it gave of the law that guards and limits the conduct of man. And so with that penalty a new power entered into life, by which Human life not a failure.

man might recover that which he had lost. Mere innocence at the best is but a passive state, without merit or reward; but when refined by trial and experience it assumes the character of *virtue*, it is a positive force in life. And while innocence is the essential quality of the primal Eden—heroic virtue is the essential feature in the paradise that is to be.

The first, we repeat, is an inheritance; the other must be earned. Men inherit wealth, and, as often quite as otherwise, they squander it; but that which they have gained by slow degrees and persistent industry, has a value, and serves a purpose it could never do without.

So Eden was *given* to man: he fell. Another lies before and beckons him in all the <small>Conclusion.</small> better moments of his life. And in the Providence that is over him, sin will lose its charm when his eyes are fully open, and sorrow will have done its work in chastening the desires. And as out of conflict cometh victory, and out of struggle a more perfect life, so by slow degrees and sometimes painful steps—God calling him upon the one hand and duty urging him upon the other —by every onward movement and every upward impulse, he shall come again to Eden by and by, and the last estate of man will be better than the first.

VIII.

ILIZATION.—CAIN AND ABEL.

"Abel was a keeper of sheep, but Cain was a tiller of the ground. . . . And it came to pass when they were in the field, that Cain rose up against Abel his brother and slew him."

"The first step in civilization was achieved by conflict, and every succeeding step of deep and lasting import has been achieved in the same way. It is the method of history."— F. H. HEDGE.

"Effort is the condition of achievement and conflict the price of victory."

VIII.

PROBLEM OF CIVILIZATION.

SOCIETY has its beginnings in a state of barbarism, and, if we may trust history, tends from time to time to relapse into its primitive condition. By barbarism we do not mean savage life, but a condition intermediate between the savage and the civilized state—a condition in which men have all the instinct, intelligence, and propensities of men without education or systematic training in any of them.

Place a child, if it were possible, away from all associates, give him shelter, food, and drink, without care or effort on his own part, and never excite the evil propensities that slumber in him, and he will grow up a respectable barbarian, having little disposition for either good or evil. Take another and surround him from the first, with circumstances that tend constantly to rouse the passions and baser propensities, and he will grow up a savage, like our Indian. Then take a third and surround him with

Three grades of society.

the appliances of cultured life; give him books and schools and intelligent companionship, and he will become civilized. These represent three distinct conditions of human life, and we readily see out of what surroundings and under what influences they severally grow.

In saying that society begins in a state of barbarism, we mean simply that humanity comes upon the stage of life in a state of nature, without training or instruction, and that it may so continue, with little knowledge beyond that necessary for supplying the most imperative wants. But the very simplest life finds means of drill and tuition in its course; means that cannot escape it, and that it cannot fail in some degree to heed.

Primitive barbarism.

Man, set down in the world without any knowledge of his surroundings, and without the assistance of a teacher, would soon become conscious of hunger and find means to satisfy the desire; and if the climate were severe, would not be long in providing some protection against the inclemencies of the weather. Then, as appetite would keep him on the alert, he would begin to exercise his ingenuity; would decoy animals and trap them, and anon would fashion weapons for slaying them. All these come in the course of nature, and require no other motives

Learning by experience.

than those which nature herself supplies. Then, following on in the same direction, by an easy and natural process, without developing much of either good or evil quality, he might come at length to keep flocks and herds that he would drive from place to place, as pastures failed, and still be nothing but a barbarian; having developed neither the vicious qualities that make the savage, nor the higher traits that lead to the civilized condition.

While, therefore, we do grave injustice to humanity to suppose it came up primarily from a savage state, we do but follow out the plain suggestions of nature and reason alike, when we assume that the early condition of human society was that of barbarism.

This was clearly the condition of the tribes and men of which we read in the remotest histories, or in the history of the earliest times. Their chief dependence was on their flocks, and they pitched their tents from time to time where the pastures were the best. So long as men confine themselves closely to this kind of life, moving quietly and subsisting on the spontaneous productions of the earth, together with what their flocks may yield, they will not develop rapidly either the baser or the better qualities; their growth or change will not be marked either way. But if they come to subsist by plunder,

Barbarism of primeval times.

added to the chase, they rapidly degenerate in a moral sense, and are so much farther removed from civilization.

And right here, we incline to believe, is one secret of our ill success in civilizing the Indian. We forget the step that lies between the state in which we find him and that to which we would introduce him. The Indian is a savage and not a mere barbarian. If you would civilize the Indian and not exterminate him, do not think to call him from the wigwam and the chase to the sickle and the plough. The transition is too abrupt, and the change too absolute. But assign him a tract of country sufficient for flocks to roam over and gather their living from the native products of the soil, and the change from his former state will not be so great but that he will inure to it, and then it will be practicable to take the other step.

The Indian question.

But to resume our subject of discourse. If we had no written testimony on the subject we should reasonably conclude, from what we know of human nature, that the early condition of society was that which we have defined as barbarous; about equally removed from civilization on the one hand and from savage life upon the other. And now, in pursuing this subject, we encounter what seems a paradox or contradiction.

Civilized life is unquestionably the highest state; and yet the very first step out of barbarism, in the direction of civilization, leads to disputes and war. That is to say, the change from one condition to the other involves the rights of property in land, about which men and nations have been wont to quarrel, certainly ever since nations had any recognized existence.

The paradox of civilization.

And here we shall find a convenient and forcible illustration in the Bible story of Cain and Abel. "And it came to pass that when they were in the field, Cain rose up against Abel his brother and slew him."

Cain and Abel, representatives of the early race, were doubtless keepers of flocks and herds, as most primitive people were, and as many in remoter sections of the world are to-day. They represent the nomadic tribes, having no permanent abodes, but moving tents instead.

Cain and Abel as general types.

In process of time, however, Cain grew weary of this kind of life and turned his attention to cultivated fields. But Abel, not sharing this disposition, was still content to rove about and live by his flocks. So much we may gather from the account of the religious offering that each one brought.

Abel may be accounted what we should now call

a conservative; thought things well enough as they were, and was possibly annoyed at Cain's suggestion or desire for change. Cain, on the other hand, was a radical in a primitive sort of way; thought he could improve upon existing methods and devise a better way of life, than to wander always homeless, in search of fresh pastures.

And here comes in the fact so paradoxical, that that which tends to improvement, in its first inception tends oftentimes to violence.

While all men wander at their will, and no one interferes to obstruct the way, because all are equal, and no one's rights are trampled on, there is no cause of quarrel regarding land or territory. But the moment one sets himself to establish a fixed abode, which he must do to have cultivated fields—not a tent that he will move next week or even the coming year, but a permanent abiding place—he must have a little territory to himself. He must become a landed proprietor; must assume the right to certain lands and claim them as his own. He builds a fence, digs a ditch, or otherwise marks the boundary of his premises, and demands that other people shall respect his right.

Conditions of civilization.

Here is the root and beginning of all the disputed titles that occupy so much the attention of our courts. One man claims a certain tract of land

and others dispute his right. But this is the result of a condition that is inevitable, if society is ever to advance beyond its primitive level. There can be no real civilization, nothing above barbarism, without established homes; and there can be no fixed abodes, or highly cultivated fields, without lines or boundaries beyond which the public has no right to trespass.

<small>Disputed titles to land.</small>

Here, then, we have the cause of the first quarrel recorded in human history. And it has more than a personal significance. It illustrates a principle that is far-reaching and comprehensive, and is applicable to every age and every people. Abel would not consent to the restriction of pasturage implied in Cain's claim to certain lands. On the other hand, Cain did not want Abel's cattle driven across his fields. They met and quarrelled, and in the strife that followed Abel was slain.

<small>Cause of quarrel.</small>

The world has long been in the habit of regarding Cain as a depraved and desperate character, and Abel as quite the reverse; but there is no evidence either way, except in the result of this encounter. And this result was only what has been repeated so often since, and what is repeated still before our eyes, that the cruder types of society and life give way

<small>Supposed character of Cain and Abel.</small>

before the advance of higher and better types, even at the cost of violent means. Both men are represented as bringing offerings or sacrifices, one of the fruit of the field, the other of the firstlings of his flock, that is, each such as he had; which shows the one a shepherd and the other a tiller of the soil. And so far, in a moral sense, there is no difference between them.

But whatever the merits or demerits of either man, and whatever the tendency of the change in men's pursuits, from the barbarous toward the civilized, Cain is represented as condemned to a career of bitterness and fear—of public execration and self-reproach.

<small>The murderer condemned.</small>

And does not history continually repeat itself in this? The slaying of a fellow-being, save in the extremest case, marks a man in society forever. The law proscribes him and pursues him, and even though he escape judicial sentence, we think of him as a murderer still. The hand of every man is against him, and he wanders for a time at least, a fugitive and vagabond in the earth. It was so then; it is so now, and will be so as long as men prize life above everything they possess besides.

These Old Testament stories are wonderfully life-like and real, if read with some exercise of reason.

Cain went to another country to live. It is not

reasonable to suppose, after what had happened, that he could have lived among the friends and followers of Abel—if he had followers. And therefore, of necessity, he withdrew to another land, and thus effected the separation of the human family into two classes, in respect to their employments. This change was indeed a necessity if Cain was to persevere in the changed mode of life he had chosen. If he was not to go back to the barbarian level, he must have a section of country to himself. It was as much a necessity to the one class as to the other. Those who adopted agriculture could not prosper in a country given up to pasturage; and those who roved about with flocks and dwelt in tents could not live in a thickly populated community, where the best lands were occupied and tilled, any more than the Mexican vaquero could keep his numerous herds in Connecticut to-day. The one kind of society and life inevitably pushes the other out, and they must dwell apart.

The migration of Cain.

The event, therefore, of the first murder derives an additional significance from the fact that it represents to us "not merely a contest between two angry men, but between two types or degrees of civilization."

Moral of the story.

And now, leaving these typical characters for the time, let us inquire into some of the effects upon the human race, of this tendency to outgrow or rise above the habits and modes of the barbarian.

Although the idea generally prevails that nomadic life is favorable to physical strength and valiancy in battle, all history and observation go to show the contrary. It is the more educated and the better disciplined that win the day, in any but the most unequal contests. That degree of civilization which best advances the interests and attainments of men, at the same time best defends them against the assaults and devices of all inferior grades.

<small>The better qualities win.</small>

In the middle ages, in Europe, when people were divided into tribes and feudal clans, their leaders, by the ill-requited labor of the masses, built great castles on such points as were easily defensible; and then, whatever depredations they might commit on the community without, they were always safe in these strong and inaccessible retreats; because an army, however numerous, could make no head against the massive walls with such weapons as were in existence.

But a German chemist, quietly experimenting in his laboratory, invented an explosive substance since known as gunpowder; and straightway these robber strongholds became untenable. They could withstand an attack

<small>Gunpowder and the castles.</small>

with slings and arrows and an occasional catapult, but not a cannonade. And to-day all over central and southern Europe are the wrecks of these old castles, telling their pregnant story of a condition of society that was but is no more. Gunpowder often serves an evil purpose, but it was a contribution of science at the first, which rendered a most important service to society, because it delivered the multitude from the control and depredations of a class of men who lived by plunder, and regarded no man's rights save their own. Here the contest was between intelligent invention and brute force; between the castle builder and the powder maker. And though the former may at first be the stronger, the latter in the end will win.

Again, this conflict is sometimes between mere mental activity and *moral* force. And here under ordinary circumstances the latter bears the palm; for while a mere adventurer may have dash — may be reckless and even desperate, it is only the man of moral courage who is really brave. This has a good illustration, as we think, in the contest of the Roundheads and Cavaliers of England in the time of Charles I.; for the question was substantially, whether the people had any rights that the king was in duty bound to consider. The royal troops were better fed, better armed, and better mounted than their opponents, but it was Cromwell's steady discipline, and the moral purpose of his men, that won at Naseby and Marston Moor.

So we might go through history; but we only wish to indicate on this point, the general proposition, that the higher aim and purpose, if steadily pursued, wins against the meaner; and before any measure that tends to develop and subserve the interest of the human race, that which hinders it must fall.

In the case of Cain and Abel, the one who would hold men to a nomadic life, in which no great advancement could be made, fell before him who had devised a better way. Cain's way was better because in its course lay all the possible achievements of the world—as we shall see. Following out his ideal, he not only tilled the ground, but he built a city also, which is not said of any man before his time—and this witnessed a farther advance of human progress; for it is in the city or in the larger community that civilization attains its best estate.

What no man can do alone, many men may do together. Hence the peculiar associations and dependencies of city life. If a family make their home apart from the busy world, on some by-way, or in some secluded spot remote from neighborship, they may

Best condition of life.

have advantages in their fixed abode they could not if they moved about like the gypsies from day to day, but cannot have the best opportunities. As to schools, and church, and society, and trade, they live at a disadvantage. These can be had only when people dwell in near communities, and where whatever any man does in the way of business is a matter of interest to his neighbor and the general public, since the welfare of the whole is in some measure dependent upon each.

It is true, that a state of comparative isolation has fewer temptations than where the associations are more intimate. It is true, that with great opportunities for good come great inducements to evil ways. But the office of opportunity, and the end of true culture in a man, is to make him strong. We should deem that bodily exercise of little practical value which only enlarged the capacity of the stomach without increasing the physical strength. And so the opportunities which a better condition of life brings to a man are of little profit, unless he is man enough to make them instrumentalities of good.

By the combination of means and the union of efforts which are rendered practicable in the city or in the larger communities, invention and progress go on as they could not, were each man compelled to eke his

Division of labor.

own living from the soil, or derive it from the chase, or from wandering flocks, in the condition of nomadic life. Some men must be spared this kind of labor, that their thoughts may be given to other things, else the world would always move on the primitive plain of simple uncultured life, and little progress could be made.

Till men are divided up into trades and professions, each giving his time and thought to some particular line or department of industry, there can be no great advancement, and society does not rise above a semi-barbarous condition. And there must be somewhere and at the hands of some one a starting-point for all improvements.

Hence, among the descendants of this tiller of the ground and first builder of a city, we find Tubal-Cain, the "instructor of every artificer in brass and iron." And Jubal the "father of such as handle the harp and organ." Here is the beginning of all mechanic arts, and the root of all improvements that have since been made; and here the beginning of instrumental music, whatever form or fashion it may have since assumed. For whatever advances have yet been witnessed in the various arts, even by the present generation, from the ruder implements of frontier life, to the most finished work of the completest mechanism or the highest art, all must have had somewhere a beginning; and the condition of society at the time of that beginning, must have been such as to foster investigation in some degree, and promote invention and discovery.

This condition is best attained, as we have seen, in a large community, where the circumstances permit or demand a division of labor; so that while one works with his hands, another works with his brain, and a third in part employs them both; and thus the whole realm of nature is explored, her secrets are found out, and the forces she holds in trust appropriated to the progress of the world. Everything of material creation is laid under contribution to this one great end—the advancement of the human race. And under the impetus given by this means to human life, it assumes a new significance and stands out more boldly among the works of God, as that for which all things else were made, and which by the very extent of its possibilities gives indication of other than earthly origin and destiny.

But this view of life, when reduced to its elements, forces us back upon the first condition. The first step toward this advanced community is the permanent abiding-place for the family; but the family and the fixed abode necessitate the right of ownership in the soil, and the moment you admit the right of any one to claim one acre of land as his own, that *Returns upon the first condition.*

moment you limit the extent of territory over which any one may wander at his will. And that is what Cain and Abel quarrelled about.

It is hardly probable that either of these men had any adequate conception of the tendency and ultimate result of what he did or attempted to undo. But one of them at least, had an ideal of something different from what he saw and what he had known in the world.

The fact, however, that has fixed the attention, from the earliest record of this occurrence until now, is that violence and death came thus early in human experience from the antagonistic ideas and tendencies of men. But the fact appears alike in nature and in human life, that when we foster the good we give harbor to the bad.

Violence a condition of advancement.

The labor that prepares the soil for the waiting grain, fits it as well for the readier growth of weeds. The same stream which, properly directed, obediently turns your mill-wheel, also breaks sometimes beyond its banks and spoils your fields. The vapor that lights your dwelling so conveniently and so brilliantly, if left to escape unwittingly, brings death where but yesternight it brought light and gladness. In such close proximity are the evil and the good. It depends on how we use what nature gives us or what our industry achieves, whether it prove a blessing or a curse. It depends on what use we make of life, whether its possession is a penalty or privilege.

Here were two boys, nourished at the same breast, going out into the world, which we should think was wide enough for both; and because they had different views and aims in life, the bosom of the virgin earth was stained with fraternal blood.

A fearful fact it is; but it illustrates the world's method of advance. All along the stream of time, from then till now, conflict has preceded victory. No great achievement is ever cheaply won. No great advance is ever made except at some great cost. By violence, civilization was given its first great impulse in the world; by violence most of its great victories have been won. What then? shall we accept this method as the only one, and pursue it still? Shall we go about to kill a man when we would improve the world?

Let us keep in mind the double or conflicting tendencies in man. He starts out in life when left alone, a barbarian. He begins life in his best estate an untutored child, with possibilities both of evil and of good; and on the training and associations more than on his native inclinations, depend the life he will lead. Ignorance and brutality will fight for life. They will resist encroachments even by those who seek their good. And when these have made great advances, it is rare that their hold is loosed except by something at least approaching violence. But in the child, the better qualities yield as readily to the influences around, as the worse. Now, suppose we begin the education of the child by other than harsh means of government. There is where his education begins as pertains to human rights.

Then think how important a part violence has always played in the education of the world. The rod in the home and the school. Men went out into the world, with the idea of the necessity of compulsion, wherever one mind or power was superior to another. The thought was not to reason and persuade, but to subjugate.

We have passed, let us hope, the earlier stage of civilization and are already trying dif-
<small>Possibility of change.</small> ferent means to accomplish the great purposes of life. Violence is in good measure put away from the home. It is being banished by degrees from the public schools. It has been successfully attempted but recently in the settlement of a national dispute. The question, therefore, as to whether the method of improvement and reform can be permanently changed, is simply a question as to whether a nation can be subjected to the same rules as an individual.

If evil maintains still the master hand, then

there is no advancement except by violent means, for evil is stubborn and will resist. But if the better nature shall gain control, if the ideal becomes the real Christian life, then by easier grades and surer steps progress will hold its course. Reason will take passion's place, and advancement in the civilization of the world will be secured without the effusion of a brother's blood.

Here our discussion properly ends.

But since a principle once established finds continual illustration in history and in our observation of the world, so there are two or three reflections that come in place at this point. <small>Subsidiary questions.</small>

The first relates to a great advance that has recently been made in the direction of civilization; and the other to a certain tendency toward a retrograde movement.

1. One of the greatest steps ever taken toward a Christian civilization was in the settlement of the "Alabama Claims," in 1873, when two of the leading nations of the earth — both numerous and powerful — having an occasion of war between them, came together by their representatives, with a third party having no practical interest at stake, and with his aid, adjusted and settled their cause of quarrel without resort to any violent means. <small>Settlement of "Alabama Claims."</small>

2. The other case relates to what is known as the Communal principle—the theory that ownership of property should be common, or the title vested in the state. This is variously represented by the Socialists of Germany, the Nihilists of Russia, the Communists of France, and a nondescript class of reformers in our own country.

Communism a retrogression.

Whatever merits may be alleged of the system as a whole, it is very certain that the general adoption of the communal principle would be a return *toward* primitive barbarism. Not a return *to* it, but a step in that direction. For communism pure and simple was the original condition.

The time was when there was no such thing as personal ownership of land. And territory was probably claimed by *tribes*, or by individual leaders for tribes, before ownership of the soil was recognized as an individual right. This primitive state of things is still retained in a measure in some European countries.

In parts of Russia, according to a recent French writer on "Primitive Property," the village or commune owns the land. To each adult is allotted a portion on which he may work and get his living, paying a certain percentage into the public treasury, though he can never possess the land in fee simple. He cannot

Communal property in Russia and Switzerland.

sell it, and there may be from time to time a redivision.

In certain cantons of Switzerland, the *commune* possesses the land, and is responsible for roads, schools, and police. Each head of a family is entitled to garden-ground enough for vegetables, fruit, and flax or hemp for household use. He is also entitled to the pasturage of two cows in the mountain meadows, and wood from the common forest. And for these privileges he pays a definite sum into the public treasury. And while to many people this seems at a distance, quite an Arcadia, the effect may be seen in the small accumulations of wealth in those cantons and the almost entire lack of individual enterprise.

Conclusion. The truth is, the moment we take from the individual the right of ownership in the soil, that moment we take from him the chief incentive to productive industry. And taking from him the personal advantage of his own skilled labor, is taking away the incentive to do the best work.

The idea of a state of society in which all men shall be equal in point of ownership, whether a man is industrious or indolent — whether he is skilled or unskilled, is purely visionary and practicably impossible. There may be grave inequalities and serious faults in society as it exists at present. Merit may not always be adequately rewarded, and impracticable genius may often find itself distanced by persistent mediocrity; but the disorder is not to be remedied by a defiance of the very first principles of justice or a disregard of the rules that govern all intelligent competition. And the best state of society to which we can hope to attain is that in which every man may profit by his own industry, his own intelligence, and his own enterprise as well.

IX.

LURE OF PRIMEVAL SOCIETY.

"The wickedness of man was great . . . And the earth was filled with violence."

> "Knowest thou not all germs of evil
> In thy heart await their time?
> Not thyself, but God's restraining,
> Stays their growth of crime."
> —WHITTIER.

> "One mischief entered, brings another in;
> The second pulls a third, the third draws more,
> And they for all the rest set ope the door;
> Till custom takes away the judging sense
> And to offend scarce seems an offence."

IX.

FAILURE OF PRIMEVAL SOCIETY.

THE first experiment of human society ended in disaster. Such is the written testimony — such the not unreasonable inference to be drawn from what we know of human nature, when left comparatively to its own suggestion and direction. Education is a plodding process. Human wisdom is a thing of slow growth, and in the most favorable conditions has but a partial following. *Human nature.*

The boy left to choose his own companions and follow his own inclinations goes to ruin. The patient watchfulness of parents and faithfulness of teachers do not always suffice to secure a different result.

The infancy of the race was much the same in many points as that of the individual, and must be accordingly considered.

Left first to unguided inclination, it showed a facility in evil growth not manifested in its tendency toward better things. The savage outran the saintly qualities in the earliest development of the race; in the first changes from the barbarian level upon which, as shown in a preceding lecture, society began. Nor was this fact an abnormal one in human life. All along the line of history it appears that the evil in man, if not most potent, has shown itself of quickest growth.

<small>Growth of evil.</small>

How many of the discoveries and inventions of men were made to serve some evil purpose before they were turned to good account. The discovery of iron, with the method of reducing it, opens perhaps the widest field of useful industry in the whole history of the world. Strike that from the sum of human achievement, and nine tenths of all our machinery and useful implements goes with it. And yet the sword was shapen before the ploughshare, and men learned more deadly ways of fighting before they learned better methods of cultivating the soil, or of appropriating human skill and labor. And even to this day it depends entirely upon the use we make of any new discovery, whether it prove a blessing or a curse.

These reflections are in some sense preparatory to what we shall have to say in this discourse, of the flood, by which primitive society came to its disastrous end. To make our way clear we must consider the condition to which society had actually come, at the time of this extraordinary event.

Both poetry and tradition are given to representing the early existence of man as a golden age of purity and innocence—of prosperity and peace. The story of Eden, as interpreted in the lecture on man, showed him as having a golden day of innocence to begin with, but falling early into disobedience and rapidly into strife. And, alas, for poetry and imagination—for tradition and romance, the earliest traces we find in fossil, of man upon the earth, are associated with implements of war; as if one of the first things men learned to do was to fall into deadly quarrels, and then fight them out. *Romance of history.*

But this need not surprise us when we are told that the second man, whose name comes down to us, was a fratricide. The story that the fossils tell us give an air of plausibility as well as probability to this account. *Early condition of society.*

And we might readily conceive without any definite record, to what condition early society would be likely to come, with such a beginning as Adam made, and such a following as Cain; and if we choose to trace the matter farther, we shall find an indication in the wild song of vengeance and defiance that Lamech addressed to his wives.

We are not entirely unprepared, after this review, for the statement that "the wickedness of man was great, and the earth was filled with violence." Humanity seems to have started on a downward grade.

But is human nature, then, constitutionally depraved to such extent that the evil inevitably overbalances the good? No: but the evil is of far the quicker growth. Plant a garden, and leave it to itself, or without careful husbandry, and the weeds will choke out all the better plants. Recalling an illustration used before, the boy left to himself develops a readier affinity for evil than for good. A man may sink to the level of the savage more easily than he can rise to that of the philosopher or the saint. A youth may make his way to profligacy in far less time than he can fit himself for important and useful service in the world. And the same reasoning, we repeat, will apply with equal force to men in the combinations of social life. Society but expresses the sum of the influence and tendencies of the individuals composing it.

Natural depravity.

On this point we quote the substance of a striking paragraph from Dr. Hedge. The first society, committed to undisciplined instincts and native passion, without education, without experience, without ideals or examples before them, and with no authority but brute force, would almost in evitably fail for lack of moral resources; for moral ideas, and therefore moral safeguards and defences, are of slower growth.

Consider the situation of that primeval society. We may easily conceive, from what we know of human nature, how soon some sort of ambition or selfish desire would spring up among men. Ambition would breed jealousy; jealousy revenge; revenge violence and war. And this course of development of human passion would be inevitable, till men had learned to think soberly, to reason rightly, and to trace with some sort of logical sequence, their acts to their causes on the one hand, and to their consequences on the other. It seems hardly strange at all, therefore, that man should have found himself literally swamped in the slough of his own misguided passions, and that the first attempt of men to live in some sort of harmony, and with some community of interests, should have proved a signal failure.

Primeval society.

An eloquent author has said: "Let the word 'ought' be stricken from our language, with all that it implies, and civilization would be dust in a day." And one chief advantage that society has now, over that of the olden time, is that man has learned to say, "I ought," and to acknowledge and regard his neighbor's rights equally with his own.

The word ought.

If to-day, all our laws of equity, the growth of centuries, could be stricken out; all the memories of good examples and heroic sacrifices, the heritage of generations, eradicated; and all our educational, moral, religious, and refining institutions razed to the ground, how soon would men forget their obligations and discard the wisest counsel, and ambition, lust, and rapine reign supreme.

But the sense of justice and of mutual dependence and responsibility had to *grow*, and approve themselves in man's own experience. And till he had had experience, both of the evil and the good that are possible to society, he could not certainly distinguish between them, for there was neither history nor example to guide him as there is to guide men to-day.

And now, since evil in its very nature is not only self-destructive but carries destruction in its train, and as evil had come to prevail in the society of that early time, in agreement with what seem the recorded facts of history, we have characterized the first attempt at human society as a failure.

<small>Nature of evil.</small>

"And God saw that the wickedness of man was great in the earth, and that every imagination of the thoughts of his heart was only evil continually. . . And God said I will destroy man."

We shall find the Hebrew idea of God and

the method of his government woven into the narrative, as we find it in all the writings of that ancient people. The theory is that disaster, calamity, and affliction; that everything in nature or experience out of the normal course; that earthquakes and epidemics, floods and fevers, are expressions of the divine displeasure. We have learned to regard these things otherwise. But such was their understanding and interpretation. And in the wickedness of the people, therefore, which was very great, was found sufficient occasion for the flood, in which the earth was cleansed of its corruption and violence by the destruction of the life upon it. *The Hebrew theology.*

The story of the flood is briefly this: that the fountains of the deep were broken up and the clouds poured out their rain, till the earth was covered and the waters prevailed above the mountain tops, destroying the life that was on the land, except Noah and his family, with the animals gathered by them in the ark, built for their preservation. *Story of the Deluge.*

The ark, as appears, was not a boat in any proper sense, but a huge box, well proportioned for floating safely on the water, but unprovided, so far as we are informed, with oar, sail, or rudder; left to drift whithersoever it might.

According to the record it was about five hundred feet long; less than one hundred feet wide, and about thirty feet high; having a capacity it is computed, about equal to that of the steamship Great Eastern. A man in Holland some years ago constructed a vessel on the model of the ark, and found it well adapted to sustain a very great weight.

Sundry questions inevitably spring up at mention of the ark, such as, how was it possible for Noah and his family to collect specimens of all the animals—one pair of the unclean and least useful, and seven of the clean and more serviceable ones? And whether it was possible for the ark to contain so many animals with food sufficient for such a time. But let us not anticipate. The problem is not so difficult as may at first appear.

Having learned the story, let us now, according to our custom, make some inquiries in other directions.

Is there any evidence, aside from the written account, that there ever was a flood?

<small>Evidence of a flood.</small> Yes. Evidence that neither the boldest scepticism can gainsay or the sharpest criticism undermine.

The testimony is of various kinds.

1. There are traditions of a flood among many races and nations, some of which know nothing of our Bible or perhaps have never heard of it; tradi-

tions dating back to the early history of man. The Chaldees, the Phœnicians, the Persians, the Hindoos, even the American Indians, but especially the races that trace their origin to the interior of Asia, have such traditions. And though their accounts vary somewhat, they agree in the important points, that the flood was destructive of human life in general, but that a few, accounted righteous persons, were saved in some sort of boat.

And though tradition is but perpetuated rumor, and not to be depended on as decisive evidence in the absence of anything beside, it is hardly possible that a tradition so general could exist, and especially with essential points so far corresponding, unless there was some good foundation for it.

2. There is evidence in many a highland district, on many a mountain side, and even on mountain tops, that at no distant period they were under the sea; in other words, that "the waters prevailed above them."

If you will go to Montreal and climb the mountain back of that city, where workmen are digging in the park, you may find there the shells of such animals as live in the sea to-day, and that at an elevation of four hundred feet above the present level of the St. Lawrence river. There is but one way of accounting for the existence of modern marine remains at such a height, and that is, that within comparatively modern times, all that region has been covered by the sea; the waters prevailed above.

And what appears so plainly in that locality can be traced with equal certainty in various regions of the earth. There is no possible doubt of the fact.

If, then, we inquire into the cause of the flood, it may have been due to either of two causes; an unusual fall of rain, or the sinking of the land in the flooded district, and a filling in of waters from the sea. Either would be effectual in accomplishing the result. The question may be asked, is there anything analogous in modern times, to such a mode of covering the land with the sea?

Causes of floods.

Yes, though on a comparatively moderate scale. About sixty years ago a tract of land, half the size of Connecticut, at the mouth of the river Indus, suddenly sank to such extent, the sea covered part of it, and the other, from high, dry land, was reduced to swamp.

Modern examples.

Still more recently a portion of the coast of Chili sank several feet, so that the waters prevailed where, in all recorded time before, had been dry land; and at another time, a sudden upheaval of a portion of that coast made dry land of a tract that had long been covered by the sea.

And sudden changes in the level of the surface of the earth are almost always attended by long and copious rains. The clouds and the sea seem to combine to work destruction upon the earth. In the expressive language of the sacred word, "The windows of heaven are opened" on the one hand, "and the fountains of the great deep are broken up" upon the other.

It is certain, then, that floods may occur, by the operation of causes that are well understood. They have occurred, and, on a small scale, still occur.

Next comes the very important question; was the Noachian deluge universal? No.

The deluge not universal.

1. There is not water enough in the earth, the air, and clouds together to cover the whole surface of the earth, to such extent it would prevail above the mountain tops.

2. Such a flood, in such a length of time, would have destroyed every plant, if not every seed upon the earth; and there is no record of any attempt to preserve the plants from the flood; and all plant life must have begun anew, presumably by a new creation, when the deluge had subsided. Moreover, the flocks that were preserved during the prevalence of the waters, after they came from the ark, must have perished for want of pastures, while waiting on the barren hills for the plants to grow again.

Further, all fishes and other animals that live in fresh water, and all corals and other animals that grow in shallow water, must inevitably have perished, for the water was both salt and deep. And no mention is made of marine animals as among those for whose preservation any provision was made.

If we seem to be taking somewhat bold ground when we say the Noachian deluge was not universal, we have only to answer in reply, that we know of no scholarly critic, whatever his religious opinions or scientific training, who believes that the earth has been completely covered by a flood at any time since the creation of man; or that the time has ever been, since the mountains were reared and the beds of the sea were hollowed out, that the whole earth was under water.

Criticisms.

How, then, are we to interpret the emphatic language of the record, that "the waters prevailed exceedingly upon the earth, and all the high hills under the whole heaven were covered?" We are to follow the same rule of interpretation precisely as in other passages, with like sweeping or general phrases. A few examples will place the matter in a clear and definite light. It is said at the time of famine that sent Jacob's sons to Egypt, that "the whole

Interpretation of the record.

world came to Egypt to buy corn." Strictly speaking, but a small fraction of the world had any knowledge of such a land as Egypt. And yet the language is not misleading. It is said of David the king that he "was feared by every nation under heaven;" when probably half the nations, at the very least, were unconscious of the existence of any such man as David.

Luke says that "Cæsar gave command that all the world should be taxed," meaning of course the Roman world or empire. Paul says to the Colossians that the gospel had been preached "to every creature under heaven;" while as yet the disciples were few and the preachers but a meagre company. It seems hardly possible for the intelligent reader to mistake the meaning of these expressions. They imply a very wide, but by no means universal extent.

Similar expressions are in daily use in our common speech. We say "the whole town" was at the meeting, meaning only that the meeting was large and enlisted general interest. We say "the whole city was excited," when much the larger portion of the people had no knowledge of the exciting cause, and no feeling or interest in it. And yet no one is misled or deceived by such language. It expresses a general fact, but is by no means specific as to numbers or extent.

A possible interpretation is that the whole world then known was but a fraction of what is known to-day, and the language had a specific application to the part that was known. But we are shut up to no such exceptional interpretation. The meaning is clear enough if we but consider the common use of terms.

What, then, is the plain and reasonable interpretation of the story of the flood?

It is, that there was a flood of unusual extent; that it was destructive both to men and beasts; that a few persons with certain kinds of animals in the flooded district were preserved; and that, in accordance with the Hebrew idea of the divine character and government, the flood being a great disaster, was attributed to the divine displeasure at the wickedness of men; and that the rescued ones became the types of purity, since on the same theory, the divine favor was manifestly upon them.

The plain meaning.

There is nothing, therefore, that need tax our credulity, much less defy our reason, in the idea that there was a flood, that it wrought great destruction, and that a few escaped its ravages.

Location of the flood.

If the Noachian deluge was not universal, in what part of the world did it occur? It is not difficult to find an answer to this question. Most of the races that have any record or tradition of a flood, trace their origin to interior or Western Asia. It is regarded now as quite certain that it was in that section of the world that man originated, and that the race scattered thence to the different quarters of the globe.

It is every way reasonable, therefore, to suppose that here is where the flood occurred. Indeed, there is ample evidence that that region has suffered seriously both by fire and flood, by earthquake and deluge, since it was first occupied by man.

Moreover, it would require but little subsidence of the land to repeat that disaster to-day, bringing in the waters of the Caspian Sea upon the north, and the Indian Ocean upon the south in such way as to flood the valleys of the Euphrates and Tigris, the Indus and the Ganges, with all their feeding streams, involving a wide continental area in destruction. Not only is this region exposed to the sea both on the north and on the south, but some portions of the interior, as the Dead Sea, lie far below the sea level now, and are only protected from inundation by the highland rims about the borders. *Possibility of another.*

One thought incidental is suggested as we pass. Whether the district covered by the flood comprehended all the earth that was then inhabited, we do not know. It is by no means improbable that the race had spread beyond its limits. And the fact that the Egyptians have no tradition of the deluge, suggests the possibility that Egypt did not share the disaster that came upon Western Asia. And the same may certainly be said of remoter portions of the world. This would make the rapid peopling of the world subsequently, more easily accounted for, and is, all things considered, the most reasonable solution of that problem.

<small>Extent of the flood.</small>

In the facts of human history, then, we find the origin of the story of the flood. In recording an affair of such tremendous moment, it could hardly be otherwise than that the account should come to be invested somewhat with the character of romance. For in this as in many other sacred stories, the facts recorded are of less importance than the lesson taught; a deeper meaning is implied than the words immediately express.

<small>The story rational.</small>

That men should have grown wicked when left without wisdom, example, or restraint is in no sense strange; and that they should have brought destruction on themselves, in consequence of vice and crime, is something we are not troubled now to understand. Only justice and truth, equity and

FAILURE OF PRIMEVAL SOCIETY. 189

honor can guarantee the existence of society. Abolish these and society disintegrates; no man trusts his neighbor, and the whole social fabric goes to rapid ruin.

But the tragedy of the flood, in different forms, has been re-enacted many times, and is passing on the stage again to-day. A nation perishes; but here and there a devoted teacher, a heroic leader, with some virtue to commend him to posterity, stands out above his nation and his age. While the nation dies he lives; and though the nation may be buried in the flood of subsequent events, he is accorded a place in the living heart of a grateful world. And here we find the moral of the lesson of the flood. *The tragedy oft repeated.*

If the time shall ever come when this nation perishes, when the very memory thereof shall have almost passed away, there are a few names, perhaps not half so many as in Noah's family, shall live; for their virtues, their courage, their fortitude and faithfulness forbid that they be forgot.

We stand upon the ruins of the Athenian Acropolis to-day. The history of the glorious times that were, seem now but the dissolving fabric of a dream. But the ghosts of such as Socrates and Plato seem still to haunt those ancient streets, and are more real to us than anything beside in the whole history of *Reflections.*

Greece. The nation was buried long ago, swept away as by a flood, but the best things in it were preserved.

And finally, if we go to Palestine and climb the dreary hills about Jerusalem, traverse the desolate Judean plains, and think of the wonders of that ancient world—of the wilderness and Sinai, of the temple and the throne—there is one figure that towers over all the rest; one life that rises above, and makes even poor and wretched Bethlehem and dilapidated Nazareth most holy ground; for there went out thence a more potent force, to shape the lives and quicken the hearts of men, than the world has ever known beside.

X.

DIVERSITY OF TONGUES.

"And the whole earth was of one language and of one speech."

"The formation of language supposes two conditions: 1. A consciousness in man of his power to produce articulate sounds. 2. A perception of the possibility of those sounds becoming the signs of his ideas."—LOCKE'S *Essay*.

"Th' invention all admired, and each how he
To be th' inventor missed; so easy 't seemed
Once found, which yet unfound, most would have thought
Impossible."
—*Paradise Lost.*

X.

DIVERSITY OF TONGUES.

WHATEVER may have been the origin of human language—whether the first created were endowed with the gift of speech, or, as seems more probable, language is the slow growth of centuries—there must have been a time when the human family was of one language and one speech. We know no argument in favor of the first theory. It is a mere assumption based on the fact that man is gifted above other animals and that he has need of speech. The other theory, namely, that language is a growth, is capable in good degree of demonstration.

Origin of language.

Place a group of animals together, and they soon come to understand each other in a sort of rude yet decisive way. Much more, two human beings, though they be of different races and different tongues, will soon communicate their sentiments and ideas to each other by articulate sounds.*

---

* Peschel states that young children of some South African tribes, left much to themselves during the long absence of parents in collecting their winter's food, develop a sort of language of their own.

The process is a very simple one. If we go back to the history of the infant race, we may suppose the first attempt to have been nothing more than a vocal impulse, having no intelligent design or intelligible meaning, but growing out of the desire for expression. Nevertheless, when found to answer a purpose, or procure some satisfactory response, it would be repeated and so grow into a habit, which would widen and extend till it comprehended a variety of sounds, each of which would have some special meaning. The same process would go on in different individuals at the same time. Each would learn to accept or imitate the other's utterances, as expressing certain ideas; and each contributing a share to the common stock, a single language would grow up and be mutually adopted.*

Growth of language.

Thus a community of people, living in the same place and in like conditions, would have one language and one speech. And so long as they continued one community, with no great variety of interests and no great diversity of aims, they would continue in the same habits of life, thought, and speech. We see this

One language at first.

---

* The theory that language is a human invention need not disturb the equanimity of the most reverent believer in the Scriptures; for it is distinctly stated (Genesis ii. 19, 20) that man gave names to the animals. They had no names till he invented and applied them

well illustrated in the unenterprising lands of the Orient, where customs of life and habit, and fashions in dress even, remain almost the same as they were thousands of years ago, though the influx and mingling of foreign elements have somewhat corrupted and changed their speech. So long as society undergoes no great changes, so long the language will undergo no important modifications. But when the first begins to change the other will soon follow, and from causes in no wise difficult to trace.

So long as a community is small and devoted largely to a common pursuit, so long there is little occasion or opportunity for change. But history and experience alike go to prove, that as a community enlarges, as its numbers increase and its business interests multiply, and especially as men of courage and ambition strike out from the old home, emigrate and lead out colonies to form new communities, as Abraham started out from Ur of the Chaldees, and Lot separated from his kinsman at the Jordan, different habits grow up and differences of speech will soon appear. *Causes of diversity.*

Although facilities of travel and communication make these things less apparent now, it is but a few years since this fact was well illustrated in our own country. We are an *Illustrations.*

English-speaking nation. And yet, a generation since, a person bred in New England found it difficult to understand a Southerner, on first acquaintance, and they of the West were quite perplexed over some peculiarities of speech of newly arrived New England neighbors.

Not only does remoteness of locality and infrequency of communication contribute to this result, but it is inevitable, as a community extends and trades and occupations increase in variety, that these differences should arise. Locality, kinds of business and habits of life must all be taken into the account. And these differences will multiply in number and widen in extent, till after a few years, people who started in life together but have been separated, will sometimes be at a loss to understand each other. In the gold mines of California a dialect grew up quite incomprehensible to one who had no knowledge of their modes of life. It is related that when Chatham, on one occasion, visited the mines of Yorkshire, he was surprised to find he could not understand at all the coal digger's speech; and, on the other hand, the statesman's polished rhetoric was but idle words in the ears of these men of brawny arm but narrow opportunities.

A consideration of much importance in this connection is that language in remote ages was unwritten, and so took no more permanent form than that which was given it in passing from lip to lip. A missionary on revisiting a tribe of Indians after an absence of ten years, found their language so changed in that brief period, he had to learn it almost anew. And a traveller in Brazil relates that his guides, from different portions of the same tribe, had marked differences of accent and inflection. *[margin: Rapid changes of unwritten language.]*

The pen and printing press now give to words some legible and lasting form, and therefore changes must be less rapid than in the early history of the race.* But in dealing with the *origin* of language, and its earliest development, we must take into account the conditions of human life in its earliest period.

Now, on the theory that the human race had a common origin, or if not that we deal with the historic portion, it is plain that at first and for a considerable period, they must have been of one language and speech. So much is clearly deducible from what we know of human society, and from the similarities that can be traced between all or most of the leading languages of the earth. For unity or affinity of language is conceded to imply unity of origin, near or remote.

---

* Mr. Henry Welsford, in his "Mithridates Minor: an Essay on Language" (London, 1848), assumes that unwritten languages change least; but recent observations do not bear out the statement.

But though there was only one language at the first, it was not possible, in the nature of things, that this should long continue.

Different tongues inevitable.

Changes in society and business introduce new words and new forms of expression, and these lead, soon or late, to new types of speech. That men came to speak different languages is a fact plainly stated in sacred history; but a fact not dependent on that statement merely for proof. We have proof in all the history of the world, and in our common observation of the world. The tongues have been confounded to such extent that it requires long study and training for persons come together from remote parts of the earth, to learn to express themselves clearly and fluently in each other's language. Even cognate languages, or those having a common root and origin, and each but a single remove from the original, will be found to possess essential differences in accent or inflection, and not unfrequently in words. Nor is anything extraordinary necessary to produce this result. It must inevitably come about, soon or late, in the very circumstances of the case.

To make the matter with which we have to do as plain as may be, let us go back somewhat in the history of the infant race.

Spreading out as they must have done from early Eden; some to seek warmer climates perhaps toward the south, and others daring the more rigorous atmosphere toward the north; some moving toward the mountains and others toward the valleys—the hunters that they might find game and the herdsmen that they might find pasturage—and still others, given to tilling fruitful fields, that they might find productive soil, it is easy to conceive how soon society must have taken on something of the tribal character. There were hunter tribes and shepherd clans, and other classes or divisions, according to the occupations of the people. Each tribe soon formed a dialect of its own, growing in part out of the prevalent mode of life, and in this differed from all the neighboring tribes.

History of the early race.

The fact that facilities of travel were meagre, and families or tribes living but few miles apart may have met but rarely, would give these differences the more opportunity to grow and become distinctly marked. Moreover, men in that day were in disposition, doubtless, very much as they are in this; and as families, communities, and tribes grew jealous of one another's strength, they would be the more inclined to live apart, and each dwell by itself: all of which would tend to make their languages more distinct.

But there were other causes tending to separate communities and build up new types of speech.

Society makes no great advances till men start up here and there, full of enterprise or full of ambition, and set themselves to attain place and power above their fellows. They conceive the plan of uniting several families in a tribe, or several communities in a state, over which they may rule; or, gathering a great number of tribes into one vast empire, as did Rurik in Northern Europe a thousand years ago.

Other causes: ambitious leaders.

First among the men of this type, of whom we have any record, was Nimrod, who "began to be a mighty one in the earth."

Nimrod.

"A mighty hunter before the Lord" he is styled. A mighty conqueror he was, for that day it seems, as well. The account given of this man in the tenth of Genesis is very brief, but full of grave significance. He seems to have conceived the idea of uniting all the tribes in a single kingdom, of which, very naturally, he aspired to be king. He saw how men were scattered abroad to the east and to the west, to the north and to the south. He saw the broad and fruitful valley of the Euphrates, and it seems to have occurred to him that this was the place for the seat of a great empire. Accordingly he went to work, with such means as were at his command. Every tribe subdued or won to his standard increased his strength and added to his fame, and in process of time he succeeded in good measure in his scheme. Like all great rulers, he sought to centralize his power and so combine these communities in one, that they should forget they had ever been separate peoples.

He built his capital with all the magnificence he could command. And when the valley of the Tigris was added to his realm he founded other great cities, and Babylon and Nineveh, both most wonderful cities of their time, are accounted among the fruits of his enterprise, skill, and power.

Babylon and Nineveh.

One daring device, attributed to him or to his people, was to rear an immense tower in the midst of the valley of the Euphrates, which should overtop any other structure ever reared by man; a tower of so great height it should serve as a beacon to all the tribes, not only in the valley but far away upon the mountains, and would tend to convince men in all time to come, that here was the mightiest power in all the earth, rivalling even the power upon the throne of heaven itself. This structure was designed not only as a monument of greatness, but as a centre about which the national pride might gather, and the national memories cluster; a sort of magnet, to draw the people together and kindle in them a popular sentiment of unity, so that there should

The great tower.

be no more desire to separate from this greatest of kingdoms; no more an inclination to be scattered abroad on the face of the earth. It was to be a sort of shrine, as Jerusalem was to the Hebrews of a later day, as Mecca is to the Mussulmen to-day.

With this bold and far-reaching design they set to work. Whether the scheme commanded at once the approval and willing aid of all concerned in it, or was carried on as the work of a master mind to which all others were in subordination, we have no certain means of knowing, nor is it important for our present purpose. But the work began. They made bricks and they used asphalt for mortar; the use of lime for such purpose then being probably unknown. The best skill of the times was doubtless brought into requisition, for the structure was designed to have something more than a transient interest and importance.

The whole affair is briefly set forth in the story of the Tower of Babel. And fortunately, where the Bible record fails us, by reason of its brevity, other history comes in to give us some detail. Ancient writers vie with one another in describing the wonders and magnificence of the tower. As nearly as can now be determined it was about five hundred feet square at the base and eight stories high, each story being of great height and the whole over

The Tower of Babel.

topping any other building ever reared by human hands. The tower was solid throughout, except the upper story, which was fitted up in royal style, for the pagan god that was supposed sometimes to come down from heaven and perch upon the high places of the earth. This is a description in brief, of the tower as it was designed to be. Whether it was completed we do not definitely know, though we are well assured it was begun and raised to a considerable height, for what are presumed to be the remains are still to be seen to-day.

As the traveller approaches the Euphrates from the west, a little south of Babylon, a huge ruin rises in the plain, and serves as a landmark for those both far and near. *Ruins of the tower.* The base is of irregular and indefinite extent, as any structure would be that had fallen to decay, but the height is about two hundred feet. The people thereabout call it Nimrod's Mountain; but it is made of brick laid in asphalt, and known thence to be not a natural but an artificial structure. And everything about it—the name, the location, the method of construction, and its very ancient date—so ancient no man pretends to fix it—combine to identify it with the tower that the people builded so long ago, under Nimrod's rule, as a testimony to all the nations of the earth.

This tower, according to traditional account and such historic record as we have, was never completed.

For the failure to carry out so magnificent a design, various causes may be assigned in the ordinary passage of events.

Possible causes of failure.

1. Nimrod was a tyrant. There can be little doubt of that; for none but a tyrant can hold crude peoples together and compel them to any toilsome enterprise. Tyrants may have their way for a time, but human nature too sorely tried will revolt, and any wide-spread revolution would stop the work.

2. The attempt to mould together in a common band, tribes of so many different tendencies and ways of life, without some underlying sentiment of unity, would be hazardous in any case, and especially so where mutual jealousies of tribes tended to make them continually suspicious of one another. It is found practically impossible to bring our Indian tribes together in a single government.

3. Kings do not always live—even if we suppose, as some do, that Nimrod represented a dynasty instead of an individual, the case is not changed in this respect. And when the place of a powerful potentate is left vacant and must be supplied, all the petty aspirants, with their several factions, come into conflict, and a degree of violence ensues that

scatters the kingdom more widely than before the attempt at unity was made. The kingdom is broken up. And the cause of rupture continues to breed animosities between the different sections, which destroy what little harmony had grown up among them, and build partition walls between them.

These are some of the causes that, in the ordinary course of human events, would tend to destroy the kingdom and scatter the people abroad again. And thus each family, tribe, or clan would be left to itself, to find its own territory, devise its own mode of life, and, as we have seen, to form a dialect and eventually a language of its own.

Let us observe before going farther the basis of fact and reasonable inference, on which our theory rests, in the particular case we have been tracing. *Conditions of the case.*

1. There were the people scattered over an extent of territory, in the immediate vicinity of the very cradle of the human race. It could hardly have been otherwise, at that early day, than that the tribes and families should have clustered in that section of the world.

2. There was Nimrod, a mighty conqueror and first among the great kings and tyrants of the earth. If no name were given, we know from all human history, that such men do now and then arise and impress themselves upon their age.

3. There was the tower in the same locality, of whose size and structure there is no chance for doubt, since the ruin still remains to tell the story for itself. On these facts and plain inferences, our theory of the great dispersion is based.

The account in Genesis gives a somewhat different version of the immediate cause of the dispersion at the Tower of Babel.

<small>The Hebrew record.</small>

And yet the essential facts of that narrative are involved and accounted for, in the theory above developed, as we think, will readily appear as we proceed. The record is of undoubted Hebrew origin, and reflects the Hebrew idea of the divine character and procedure.

The facts on which the account was based were these:

1. Here were these people living in close proximity, but unable to understand each other's speech. It seemed a divine judgment upon them for some offence.

<small>Data of the story.</small>

2. There stood the tower. The people of the region explained that the attempt had been made to build it up to heaven. It was accounted an impious as well as daring scheme. And the ready interpretation was that the consequence appeared in the curse of confusion that had come upon these scattered tribes. The Hebrew idea of the ways of God with men, supplies the only element

necessary to make the two accounts, in all essential points, the same.

Now, we return to the proposition stated in the beginning, that while there was but one language at the first, as men increased in numbers and varied in locality and occupations, their forms of speech became more and more diverse, and the result was different languages.

The multiplication of tongues had probably begun before the events of Babel. But the confusion became more decided and the differences more pronounced, by reason of the rupture of the great kingdom, and the ambitions, hates, jealousies, and bitter tyrannies resulting, which served to drive the tribes more widely asunder than they had ever been before. Diversities before Babel.

But the Babel-builders were not the only representatives of their race. We touch a principle here that reaches far and wide, and the story has been repeated many times in human history.

Nimrod is not the only conqueror who has conceived the daring scheme of uniting all the nations of the earth in one; nor the only conqueror in whom ambition has quite o'erleaped itself.

Alexander and Napoleon are names more familiar to us. Their schemes were no less audacious and scarcely less disastrous in their results. A daring game has been The story repeated.

played on the stage of Europe in very recent years. The hungry northern bear has had his giant paws almost on the prize along the Hellespont he has coveted so long. The British lion, somewhat discomfited, showed signs of war, but was appeased for the time, by a liberal share of the incidental spoils. While the master spirit of the continent looked on, from the safe distance of the German court, marking out the map of Europe as he intended it should be. Never were planned more daring schemes, and never was ambition more ambitious.

But all history proves that ambition has its limits and its checks. And that there is a Power above the world that is more than any power in the world, ought to be sufficiently apparent, in the fact that the abortive schemes of designing men are somehow turned to good account, in the progress of the human race. "All new languages," says Bunsen, quoted by Dr. Hedge, "have arisen from the breaking up of some great political bond which imposed one speech on its constituents."

Lesson of the ages.

The breaking up of the Latin empire gave birth to no less than five of the languages, that are spoken in Southern Europe now.

And this is only one of the many facts to be considered in the contemplation of this subject The youth who would accomplish anything must not remain in leading-strings, but strike out for himself. The same is true of nations as of individuals. The nations that spread out into all the earth, after the great dispersion, accomplished more in the way of discovery and invention, of enterprise and progress, than would have been possible had they remained grouped together, in any single section of the world. When Cæsar sat upon the throne, Rome was accounted mistress of the world. Discord and confusion entered in and her imperial dignity was sacrificed. But all Europe since, is peopled with nations that vie with one another, in industry and enterprise such as Rome never knew; and so the defeated schemes, of here and there a single man, promote the happiness and progress of the human race.

Conclusion.

XI.

ANTIQUITY OF MAN.

"What is man? . . .
Thou madest him to have dominion over the works of Thy hand.
Thou hast put all things under his feet."
— *The Psalmist.*

"Chronologists are agreed that about 2,000 years B.C. Abraham migrated from Mesopotamia to Canaan, and, that at this time, Egypt at least was old in civilization. Beyond this, we have no positive scale of time."—PATTISON.

. . . "Tongues, that syllable man's name,
On sands and shores, and desert wilderness."
—MILTON.

XI.

THE ANTIQUITY OF MAN.

MAN is a recent comer upon the earth; the last, indeed, of which we have any record. But in saying his coming is recent we use the word only in a relative sense. A period of time may be absolutely long, yet relatively short—short as compared with the whole lapse of time from the beginning until now.

Man the last of the Creation.

The past half century has witnessed very important changes in our chronological tables.

Archbishop Usher, of the English Church, some two and a half centuries since, taking the Bible narrative as his guide, made the period of man's occupancy of the earth, somewhere from four thousand and four to four thousand one hundred and seventy-four (4004 to 4174) years before Christ, or say, in round numbers, six thousand years to the present date. It is evident, however, to any careful reader in this day, that there are wide intervals of time in that narrative, for which no allowance is made in the

Usher's chronology.

good bishop's calculation. A descendant of David of the tenth generation, was a "son of David" as much as one of the first; and persons of small importance were doubtless omitted from the record entirely.

The vagueness and uncertainty of such calculations may be illustrated in this wise. If in some far future age, all knowledge of this country shall have faded into dim tradition, and the attempt shall be made to re-write its history, it is conceivable that the names of Washington and Lincoln may alone survive, in the list of our chief rulers. And if on that account, the reader shall conclude that the administration of the latter matched on to that of the former, and that at its close the government came to an end, it is evident he will get but a meagre idea of the times so full of interest to us. So the Old Testament record must be regarded not as a consecutive history, but a series of fragments, with wide lapses often between events there narrated in close and continuous order.

Still, men feeling a sort of security in definite dates, and little given perhaps to speculation, accepted Usher's chronology, with little question, for many years. But facts, long unconsidered or held to be of small importance, have forced a revision of opinion on the subject. Some of these facts it is our purpose to consider in this discourse.

Written history does not carry us back more than four thousand years. The Egyptian monuments — accounted the oldest structures of their class in existence — may carry us three thousand years farther. The earliest records, therefore, of such character do not go back more than seven thousand years. The best authorities, as Lepsius and Bunsen, make the period something less, while Champollion and Mariette somewhat extend it. *[The limits of history.]*

But whatever date may be assigned to the early Egyptian temples, obelisks, and inscriptions, beyond these we have no written history and no monumental records, excepting such as pertain to habitations, implements, and modes of life of a people of whose existence we have not even a tradition preserved among recent inhabitants of the world.

No existing race traces its lineage to the Cave-dwellers of Belgium, the "Kitchen-midden" men of Denmark, to the Mound-builders of America, or even to the Lake-dwellers of Switzerland. There is doubtless a connection between those ancient races and the men that live to-day, but the line is lost in a period of blank obscurity between. *[Indications beyond tradition.]*

And suppose we go back to Egypt seven thousand years ago, we do not find the human race there in its infancy. They had a language, not merely of signs but of vocal utterances—a written language, not of mystic hieroglyphs only, but of characters that may still be read; they had extensive knowledge of many useful arts, and they had a well-established form of government. Men do not leap at a bound to such condition. It took the Hebrews a thousand years, from the departure of Abraham from his early home to develop a systematic and stable government. And if it be said their captivity in Egypt hindered their progress, it is quite as reasonable to suppose that their contact with Egyptian institutions and their knowledge of Egyptian government, also helped their progress. If the process was impeded in one direction it was facilitated in another. Besides, these people had already reached the tribal condition, with a patriarchial head, before their migration began, which implies a considerable history or experience still back of that point.

If, then, we suppose the Egyptians to have lived under an established monarchy, and to have built and inscribed monuments seven thousand years ago, it is evident the infancy of the race, and even of that particular people, must have dated far back of that There had been time to invent, construct, and sys-

Remote infancy of the race.

ANTIQUITY OF MAN. 217

tematize language; to invent, discover, apply, and improve some of the arts; to try various rude experiments of government in family, clan, and tribe, and to pass from dependence on the chase to the care of flocks, and from the nomad's tent to the fixed habitation.

In any attempt to trace this remote condition of mankind the ordinary means of investigation fail us utterly. There is neither document nor monumental record, and even the dim light of tradition is wanting. *Failure of common data.*

Our dependence must be upon the manifest changes in the condition of the human race, knowing those changes to be wrought by slow degrees, or upon changes in the earth, as to climate, surface deposits, and forms of life, since man's earliest appearance. If, for instance we find the remains of man—either skeleton or handicraft—in cave-deposit, shell-heap or peat-growth, associated with the bones of animals long since extinct, we are justified in assigning a remote antiquity to such remains. If clear indications of man are found in rock or undisturbed gravel, at a given depth below the surface, and we find means to determine the rate of deposit of such formation, and the length of time since the deposit ceased, we may calculate with moderate certainty the length of time since such men lived.

We must use caution, however, not to attach a definite value or measurement to processes or agencies which by their very nature are variable, and therefore indefinite. The rate of river erosions, for instance, on which much reliance is sometimes placed, varies according to the quantity of water and rapidity of the current; and these may change from year to year, still more from one century to another. Likewise, the growth of peat and accumulation of stalagmitic crusts, vary between wide limits in different localities, and from time to time in the same place. Again, great changes of climate, and entire change of the types of vegetable and animal life, may be regarded as indicating extended periods of time, but we do not sufficiently understand the causes of these changes to make them the basis of definite calculations. Indeed, it is quite evident that such changes are far from uniform in their rates of progress.

Necessity of caution.

There are certain indications, however, that may be studied with more confidence. These are found chiefly in peat-bogs, cave-deposits, shell-heaps, and in remains of ancient habitations in Switzerland known as lake-dwellings.

Our dependence.

But to facilitate our study let us lay out our work more definitely; considering first the geologi-

ANTIQUITY OF MAN. 219

cal divisions of the Quaternary Age, and then the periods into which the era of man's existence is usually divided.

The geologist commonly divides the Quaternary Age of the earth's history into three periods, the Glacial, Champlain, and Terrace. For convenience in our discussion we have added a fourth, the Present period corresponding to what Prof. B. F. Mudge, of Kansas, has styled the Delta period, in allusion to the deposits now forming at the mouths of great rivers, as the Mississippi, the Nile, and the Ganges.* Periods of the Quaternary Age.

In the first, or glacial period, all or the greater part of this continent, as far south as the Ohio River and the southern line of Pennsylvania, was covered with a great depth of ice, as shown by glacial scratches, and by erratic boulders scattered here and there over the country, at a wide distance from the beds in which they originated. And in Europe the ice prevailed as far south as Northern Italy. This was, of course, a period of extreme cold. There could have been little, if any life, either animal or vegetable, in the higher latitudes, and man could have lived only along the skirts of the glacier, or after it had retreated. Glacial period.

---

* The reader is here referred to the upper section of the Chart affixed to the Sixth Lecture. Page 123.

The animal kingdom was represented by the Mammoth and Rhinoceros, which had survived from an earlier period, the Cave-bear and Hyena, and somewhat later by the Reindeer; all of which have been long extinct, save the Reindeer, which has migrated to a northern clime, following close, as would seem, upon the receding ice.

Succeeding the Glacial, or "Great Ice" period, came the Champlain, marked by a lower general level of land, a consequent wider extent of sea and warmer climate.

Champlain period.

In this period the glaciers melted in the regions now covered by the temperate zones, retreated northward or toward mountain tops, leaving their vast accumulations of rocks, gravel, clay, sand, and the like, to which the geologist applies the general name of Diluvium or Drift. The animals of this period differed in a marked degree from those of the preceding, as the changed climate would lead us to expect, and included the huge sloth-like Megatherium, with a considerable number that still survive, as the lion, tiger, wild boar, ox, horse, and deer. There were monkies also in Asia and marsupials in Australia.

Following the Champlain came the Terrace period, during which the land gradually rose again, the sea withdrew to its present limits, and the successive levels called

Terrace period.

Terraces were formed along the rivers by the gradual withdrawal of the streams to narrow and deeper channels. Some fine examples of the terraces of this period may be observed at Walpole and Hanover, N. H., and elsewhere along the valley of the Connecticut. The climate again had undergone a change; was colder than that of the Champlain, but milder than that of the Glacial epoch. The animals were similar to those that live to-day, and need not therefore be described or named.

Now, as to the bearing of these facts upon the subject we have in hand. There is no doubt of the existence of man from the earlier Champlain through the whole of the Terrace period, to the present. There is little question but that man lived in southerly latitudes in the latter part of the Glacial period. Beyond that we must proceed with extreme caution. But let us not anticipate.

Having noted particularly the different geological periods into which the Quaternary Age of the earth is divided, let us mark next the periods into which it is customary to divide the era of man's existence; observing that the two series are entirely independent of each other.

Archæologists distinguish four different periods in the existence of the human race, according to the degree of advancement in art, namely: *The Era of Man.*

1. The *Palæolithic*, or Rough Stone Age.
2. The *Neolithic*, or Polished Stone Age.
3. The Bronze Age, and
4. The Iron Age.

Some authorities recognize still other distinctions and mark other divisions. But the above is very simple and sufficiently exact for our purpose.

<small>The Paleolithic Age.</small> The Rough Stone Age marks the rudest stage of man's existence; when arrows, knives and other implements of the chase and for domestic use, were roughly shapen from hard stone, chiefly flint and argillite.

<small>The Neolithic Age.</small> The Polished Stone Age marks a period of some advancement upon the condition of the former, when men had learned to smooth and polish their implements; and they employed a greater variety of hard stones, including porphyry, greenstone, and occasionally obsidian and jasper.

<small>The Bronze Age.</small> The Bronze Age marks the early use of metals in the arts—not the earliest, certainly, for men must have used copper before they learned to mix it with tin, producing the alloy known as bronze. But where metal was used in the same way as stone, that is, without fusing and moulding, the people must be regarded as still in the Stone Age.

The Iron Age marks the higher civilization,

when men, having learned mining and smelting, began to produce that most useful of all the metals. Wherever the history of man has been definitely traced, he seems to have passed through these several stages, or to be passing through them now. Where iron is in use at present, metals more easily obtained were once employed, and before that, stone served the purpose, either rudely fashioned or smoothly and neatly shapen, according to the knowledge and skill of the workmen. *The Iron Age.*

It must be borne in mind that the "Stone Age" does not indicate any particular period of the earth's history, but a certain grade of civilization or degree of advancement among men. The Stone Age in France and that in Denmark may have been contemporaneous, or they may have been wide apart. And while we speak of the Stone Age in Europe as very remote, the American Indians were in the Stone Age less than three centuries ago, and some of the South Sea Islanders are passing through that period now. *"Stone Age" not a geological distinction.*

In some sections of the world the advance has been much more rapid than in others; and there have been cases, no doubt, of relapse from the higher conditions of society to the rude and barbarous state. But this does not effect the fact that the general tendency and direction has been from the lower toward the higher levels, in skill and knowledge and in the use of the arts.

And now, what aid will these considerations render us in tracing man's antiquity? Let us see.

A gradual advancement. If, in a country long inhabited by a highly civilized people we find relics of the Stone Age, we are compelled to assign to them a remote antiquity; for the reason that men do not pass rapidly, or in any brief period from one age and condition to another, much less through the several grades from the lowest to the highest.

The people of the Paleolithic Age must have learned by slow degrees to smooth and perfect their spears and hatchets, and it was only when the rude implements had given way to the better workmanship, that the people were fairly in the Neolithic or age of polished stone. The periods thus overlap each other. And a like gradual advance no doubt marked the changes to the ages of Bronze and Iron.

Remains of extinct animals. Again, when with buried implements we find the remains of animals known to have been long extinct, we have further evidence of the remoteness of the period in which such implements were made; for neither the plants nor the animals of the world change suddenly, except in case of some abrupt and violent change in the climate or other physical condition of the earth; and geology does not discover any such convulsive change within the period of man's existence.

The fact that plants and animals adapted to a tropical clime once occupied the middle latitudes, and again that the reindeer, now found in Arctic regions, once wandered to the south of France, indicate remarkable changes of climate, and we may suppose, equally great changes of animal and vegetable life. But we have no reason to suppose these changes to have been cataclysmal; rather, that they were gradually wrought, and therefore covered a vast period of time.

But let us note a few facts bearing directly upon the subject.

The first marked and conclusive evidence of the great antiquity of man—we mean greater than that of Usher's chronological reckoning—was found in the ancient gravel beds along the valley of the river Somme, in northern France. Here Boucher de Perthes began his researches, and here Lyell and other English scientists followed. In the gravel, which still lay undisturbed, were found flint implements, evidently the work of human hands; and as the river had slowly carved out its channel to the depth of sixty feet since those deposits were made, it was evident the implements represented a remote period of time. They were the work of the "Stone Folk"—in other words, belonged to the Stone Age.

In caves of France, Belgium, and England have been found human remains, either bones or implements, under accumulations of cave-earth and stalagmite, that indicate a great lapse of time. They are usually associated with remains of the cave-bear, hyena, mammoth, and other animals, most of which are now, and have been for a long period extinct. These caves were places of refuge and probably habitations of primitive man. Thither they carried game for food, and animals sought the refuse they left behind. And now the remains of man and beast lie confusedly together.

The Cave-dwellers (Troglodytes).

Sometimes the caves were used as burial-places, and charred wood, the remains of fire used in preparing the funeral feasts, or possibly for purposes of cremation, are found near the entrance. Skeletons are rarely obtained in sufficient state of preservation to admit of exact investigation. Two or three skulls, however, have attracted so much attention as to demand some special mention.

The "Neanderthal Skull," discovered in 1857, beneath a depth of four or five feet of earth or loam, in a cave near Düsseldorf, was regarded as of a low type bearing some resemblance to that of an ape. Some ardent and incautious evolutionists sought to identify it with the " Missing Link." But Mr. Darwin, after a careful examination, pronounces it "very well developed and capacious," indeed, not far below the average European skull. Virchow considers it of very moderate dimensions, but unquestionably a human skull. And Huxley bears his testimony to the same effect. It belonged, doubtless, to a rude savage—probably a representative of the Rough Stone Age.

At Cro-Magnon, in the south of France, in 1858, in a "rock-shelter" formed by a broad, overhanging ledge of limestone in a ravine, were discovered the skeletons of three men, a woman, and a child, all in a moderate state of preservation. One of these men, now familiarly designated as "the old man of Cro-Magnon," was about six feet in height, superior to the Neanderthal man in cranial development, but bearing such close resemblance to him as to warrant the conclusion that they belonged to the same race.

With these remains were found spears and arrow-heads of flint, that betray some advancement in art, being well shapen and comparatively smooth, and also less massive than those belonging to the crudest age. There were also a few ornaments or trinkets of shells and ivory. These people must be regarded as belonging to the latter part of the *Paleolithic*, or possibly the opening of the *Neolithic* Age.

Other noted caves or rock-shelters are found at Aurignac and Mentone, France; at Enghis, Belgium, and at Torquay and Brixham, England. But their revelations are much the same. They represent man as living in a rude condition, and fighting his way in the world, against wild beasts, including the mammoth and hyena, with weapons fashioned usually with little skill, from flint and other refractory stones

The "Kitchen-Middens."
Other evidences of the antiquity of man are found in *shell-heaps*, the refuse of feasts. These have been more carefully studied in Denmark than elsewhere, and are there known as "Kitchen-Middens." Primitive man seems to have gathered in great numbers on the sea-shore, to feast on the oyster, mussel, and periwinkle, together with a few aquatic birds and such fishes as might be taken in shallow water, and to have left behind these indications of his presence.

Some of these heaps are of prodigious size, considering their origin, and must have been centuries in accumulating. Steenstrup describes them as a thousand feet long and ten feet high.

The fact that the *Kitchen-Middens* are not

found on the western coast of Denmark, where the ocean is slowly eating away the land, and that they are found sometimes seven or eight miles back from the shore, on the eastern side, where the water is comparatively quiet, and the land is slowly building out, affords some indication of the length of time since they were made.

And the additional fact that the oyster has almost disappeared from the Baltic Sea, and that the cockle and periwinkle, which remain, are much smaller than those whose shells are heaped upon the shore, implies a great change in the water of that part of the sea. It is less salt than formerly; That is to say, the adjoining land is higher and the influx of fresh water greater. And still there has been no sudden change in the land level of that portion of the earth in recent ages. The change was slow, and hence must have covered an extended period.

Again, in the *Kitchen-Middens* are found flint knives, arrow-heads, and the like, both rough and polished, but nothing of metallic nature. They are of the Stone Age.

In the same country are the famous *Skovmoses*, or Peat-beds, which afford perhaps the most indisputable of all evidence of the great antiquity of man. These beds of moss and other plants which have changed to

<small>The Peat-Mosses.</small>

peat, occupy depressions in the general level sometimes known as boulder-pits, and have a depth in some instances of thirty feet. The age of the peat-beds has been estimated at four to five thousand years, but competent authorities add that it may be four times as great. The growth of peat is usually very slow, but it sometimes accumulates with considerable rapidity. We cannot safely judge, therefore, of the age of a bed by its depth or extent.

We have, however, in the Danish peat-beds, one indication not usually met with in such formations.

In the peat, at various depths below the surface, are prostrate trunks of trees, that have evidently grown upon the borders of the bog and fallen in. In the lower beds, two to five feet from the bottom, is the Scotch fir, a tree not now found indigenous in Denmark, and that does not flourish when transplanted there. Some of the trunks are two to three feet in diameter, and their number indicates that they were at one time the prevailing forest tree.

Fossil trees in the peat.

Above these, and still at a considerable depth below the surface, are trunks of oak, of still greater size, that in like manner must have grown upon the banks and fallen into the bog. This tree is scarcely known in Denmark now.

At a still higher level is found the beech which

is the common forest tree of the country to-day. Changes of vegetation imply changes of climate.

Here, now, are three classes or species of prevailing forest trees, implying so many changes of climate or other physical conditions. Moreover, it is scarcely conceivable that such a change could have been effected in a single generation. There were probably several generations of each kind of trees. Some idea, then, may be formed of the lapse of time since the peat-beds began to accumulate. There was a growth of Scotch fir, supplanted at length by the oak, and that in turn by the beech. And the beech not only occupied the ground at the time of the Roman invasion, almost two thousand years ago, but is the tree of Danish tradition. In other words, we have no trace either in history or tradition of the period of the earlier growths.

But what bearing have these facts on human history? Just this. In the lower beds of peat are found implements of man's workmanship — flint arrows — under the trunks of fir, in such position as they could not have reached by simply working their way downward through the moss, as pointed implements may sometimes do. These arrows were lost in the bog while the Scotch fir was growing on the bank. Man must, therefore, have inhabited the country at the time. In higher layers of the peat are found

Fossil implements in the peat.

other implements, both bronze and iron, which mark the different periods into which the age of man is divided.

Quatrefages states that the Scotch fir in the peat-beds may be regarded as corresponding to the Stone Age, the oak to the Bronze, and the beech to the Iron. But this statement must be taken with some allowance.

Once more in the same line of evidence. The fishermen of Neuchatel and other parts of Switzerland had long been annoyed by a mysterious entangling and breaking of their nets by obstructions, at the bottom of the lakes, that could not be discerned.

<small>The Swiss Lake-dwellings.</small>

The draining of a portion of one of the lakes, in the winter of 1854, brought to light a number of piles or posts driven into the mud, which had evidently been shapen for the purpose and placed there by human hands. About these timbers, at various depths below the surface, were found stone implements, both rough and polished, together with pieces of rude pottery shaped by hand, but without the aid of the wheel, and known thence to antedate the Roman period.

Further examination revealed the fact that these piles had sometime served the purpose of foundations for human habitations, built out over the lake, and connected with the shore in some cases, by a sort of causeway. This discovery stimulated exploration, and it now appears that such dwellings were once common in Switzerland. And the farther discovery of the bones of animals, both extinct and recent, wild and domesticated, also of canoes and fishing tackle, and in western Switzerland of bronze as well as stone implements, indicates that the existence of the lake-dwellers covered an extended period of time, and that from first to last, considerable advances were made in the arts of civilization. They built their houses in these novel positions for safety against the incursions of savage neighbors. Oftener than otherwise there seems to have been no direct communication with the shore, except by boat, or possibly by drawbridge, of which no traces now remain.

Herodotus describes such dwellings in Thrace twenty-five hundred years ago. Remains of such have been found in some of the boggy lakes of Ireland; and similar buildings are found to-day in some of the islands of the South Pacific. The earlier lake dwellings of Switzerland must be assigned to the Stone Age, and the later to the Age of Bronze.

These evidences, the lake-dwellings, the kitchen-middens, peat-bogs, and cave-deposits tell one story—that man existed on the earth far back of the historic period. But, it will

Value of the evidence.

be observed, we have not in any of them the data for definite calculations in years.

Suppose we admit that they fully justify the usual division of the human period into the several ages designated as Stone, Bronze, and Iron, we have no clue, in this fact, to the length of time required for man to pass through any one of them. Suppose we find, in the middle layers of peat, trunks of oak trees three hundred or five hundred years old; we do not know whether the period of the oak covered one generation or many.

What, then, is gained by the examination of such evidence?

Just this. It serves to establish the fact of man's remote origin; not to measure the period of man's occupancy of the earth in years, or even in centuries, but only to show it to be far beyond that formerly assigned.

We have means, however, for an approximate estimate.

Let us now compare the periods of the human era, or the Age of Man, with the periods of the Quaternary formation in geological history; bearing it in mind, as before stated, that there is no *necessary* correspondence between them. The two relate to different subjects; nevertheless they are intimately related to each other.

<small>Quaternary and human periods.</small>

ANTIQUITY OF MAN.

If the remains of man and those of particular animals are found together in any considerable quantities, and especially in several different localities, it is reasonable to presume that such men and animals inhabited the earth at the same time. There may be an exceptional case, now and then, where remains from widely different periods have become accidentally mingled; but such cases must be rare.

We have found, with the earliest relics of man's workmanship, the remains of the mammoth, and one or two other animals long since extinct. We have also found the mammoth and its brute companions to have lived in the Glacial period. But because man and the mammoth were at one time together upon the earth, it does not of necessity follow that their advent was contemporaneous. The appearance of the mammoth may have long preceded that of man, as man has certainly long survived the mammoth.

Man and the Mammoth.

Fossils of this huge animal clearly indicate that some species lived before and during the Glacial period; but it was only after it had passed its meridian that man appears to have disputed its sovereignty of the earth.

A careful examination of the whole subject leads us to the conclusion, that man appeared in

Europe during the *latter part of the Glacial period;* or certainly not earlier than that period of partial recession of the ice, sometimes designated as the *Interglacial* epoch.

<small>Man post-glacial.</small>

It is possible that explorations in the tropics may yet set the mark farther back, but there is no evidence in Europe or America that warrants a remoter date.

Such are the conclusions—so far, at least, as Europe is concerned—of the Anthropological Society of London, according to the Report for 1878. And Prof. Huxley, in his address before the British Association, at Dublin, in the same year, reaches substantially the same conclusion.

We are well aware that some archæologists claim a higher antiquity for the race, but on grounds that seem to us inconclusive; such as the occurrence of bones considered human in Tertiary deposits; marks of sharp instruments upon the bones of animals used for food, with the presence of sharp flints and charred wood in the same deposits.

<small>Claims of higher antiquity.</small>

With reference to these it must be said:

1. Bones found in the Ohio valley, in the early part of the present century, and confidently pronounced human, were, on examination by competent authority, found to belong to the frame of one

ANTIQUITY OF MAN. 237

of the large quadrupeds. And several such mistakes have been made, even by men of science, in the past two hundred years.

2. Markings on bones, resembling those made by sharp instruments, may have been produced by the teeth of animals that fed upon the remains.

3. Many sharp fragments of flint, hastily pronounced the result of human workmanship, have been found to be natural fragments, and may be matched along the chalk beaches of England and elsewhere where flint abounds.

4. Human bones and flint implements have, in some cases, been accidentally and confusedly mingled with deposits of an earlier date.

5. The presence of charred wood is not always a positive evidence of the presence of man. No other animal uses fire, but lightning played its hazardous freaks long before man existed on the earth, and spontaneous combustion was a possibility of former as it is of recent times.

A skull is reported to have been found in volcanic breccia of the Tertiary Age (Pliocene period), in Calaveras County, California, associated with gold-bearing gravel. But it is now deemed quite probable that the auriferous gravels, or gold-drift, of California, belong wholly to the Quaternary Age. And Prof. LeConte regards the later lava deposits also as

The California skull.

Quaternary, perhaps as late as the Champlain period.

Moreover, that Calaveras discovery has a secret history not inaptly travestied in Bret Harte's "Society upon the Stanislaus." The skull was not seen *in situ* by any scientist, and any theory based upon that as a "pliocene skull" must be taken at great hazard.

<small>Summing up the evidence.</small> Then, as to the testimony of cave-deposits, peat-beds, and the like, of which we have already spoken in some detail.

The gravel beds of the river Somme have been marked as of very ancient date. But the fact that the Somme has cut its way through the glacial drift into the chalk or Cretaceous rocks, and that these ancient gravels lie on the slopes of the chalk, proves conclusively that the cutting has been done since the drift was deposited, and, therefore, since the close of the Glacial period. The shell-heaps certainly cannot be assigned an earlier date, for had they existed before, they would have been inevitably crushed and swept away by the movement of the ice.

And whatever age may be assigned to the Danish peat-beds, they occupy cavities or depressions in the surface, believed to have been scooped out by the action of the glaciers, and must hence have accumulated since the glaciers passed away.

The Swiss lake-dwellings are variously estimated at from thirty-three hundred to six thousand years old; and few authorities would venture to assign to the glaciers a date so recent. In certain caves human remains have been found beneath stalagmitic crusts three to five feet in aggregate depth; and in one case that has been carefully observed, the rate of accumulation is said not to exceed one sixteenth of an inch in a century. At this rate a deposit of five feet would require the enormous period of ninety-six thousand years. But there is no evidence that the rate of accumulation has been uniform. And the fact that in a cave at Gibraltar, eighteen inches of stalagmite has been shown to have accumulated in less than six hundred years, and that according to Prof. Winchell, stalactites sometimes grow in the lead caves of the West, at the rate of one foot in a single year, shows the utterly unreliable character of all estimates based on the rate of progress of such formations. And yet on some such precarious evidences are all the arguments for the pre-glacial existence of man based. We submit, that they are not reliable, satisfactory, or conclusive.

The question, then, as to the date of man's advent turns upon the date of the disappearance of the glaciers from the middle and lower latitudes.

As the glaciers that once overspread Europe as far south as the Pyrenees and Italian Alps, withdrew toward the north, by reason of the softening climate, man followed; perhaps not close upon their brink, but not far behind. His companions were the cave-bear and the mammoth, and later the reindeer and the dog. The mammoth and his brute companions have long since disappeared; not a single specimen having lived, so far as we have any evidence, within the historic period. We know of them only by their fossil remains. The reindeer is not extinct, but has migrated from the middle latitudes, following close upon the retreating glacier, and is found now only in Arctic regions.

Man's relation to the glaciers.

Arrived at this conclusion the question changes form.

How long since the Glacial period?

Some attempt has been made to estimate the time by the rate of river erosions, which we have already found to be variable, and not, therefore, wholly reliable.

Date of Glacial period.

For instance, it is evident that the Niagara River has cut its present channel since the close of the Glacial period, for the old channel, *filled with glacial drift*, may still be discerned, leading from near the whirlpool, to a point on the lake several miles west of the present river-mouth.

The rate of recession of the falls has been variously estimated at from one inch to one foot per annum. By the latter estimate the channel, now six miles long, would be carved out in thirty-one thousand years. According to the former, it would require three hundred and eighty thousand. This gives a wide range for differences of opinion. *Recession of Niagara Falls.*

Other estimates have been based upon the accumulation of deposits in some of the Swiss lakes and erosion of river beds, since the disappearance of the glaciers from the lowlands of Switzerland. But the figures range from eight thousand to one hundred thousand years. And M. Quatrefages, who quotes these estimates, blandly suggests that the truth doubtless lies between these two extremes. We reach no safe conclusions from such data. They may indicate more or less.

We shall find the most satisfactory estimates to be based upon astronomical science. The relations of the earth and sun undergo periodic changes, due to the precession of the equinoxes and variations in the eccentricity of the earth's orbit. *Evidence from Astronomy.*

According to Prof. Croll, of Scotland, there was, about *eighty thousand years ago*, a period of intense cold, when a great part of the northern hemisphere was shrouded in ice. This was the era known in Geology as the Glacial period.* And this gives us the most definite clue to the antiquity of man. If we suppose the glaciers to have been at their height eighty thousand years ago, the date of their disappearance must have been some thousands of years later, for great depths of ice do not fade away in a night, nor, if we may trust recent observation, in many centuries.

But we are content to leave the matter here. Man may have been upon the earth, if the assumed data of the glaciers is correct, sixty or seventy thousand years. But there is no sufficient evidence that he lived before the ice cap had receded from the region in which his earliest remains are found.

<small>Antiquity of man.</small>

---

* We have purposely avoided all reference to any other than the one ice period. There may have been many in the course of the earth's history; but it is with the last only that we have to do.

XII.

Remains of Ancient Civilization.

" Behold ! what works were these in times of old ? "

" A nation departing, leaves this trace behind.

" I wandered by a goodly town
  Beset with many a garden fair,
  And asked of one who gathered down
  Large fruits, how long the town was there.
  He spoke, nor chose his hand to stay ;
' The town has stood for many a day,
  And will be here forever and aye.' "

" Some thousand years went by, and then
  I saw the self-same place again.
  And lo ! a country wild and rude ;
  And, axe in hand, beside a tree,
  The hermit of that solitude,
  I asked how old the wood might be.
  He said, ' I count not time at all ;
  A tree may rise, a tree may fall,
  The forest overlives us all.' "

—Arabian Tales.

XII.

REMAINS OF ANCIENT CIVILIZATION IN NORTH AMERICA.

WHEN, on an October morning in 1492, an adventurous mariner looked out from his gallant little ship, upon the shores of this western world, he supposed it to be none other than the eastern border of the older continent. And the people he called Indians, because he supposed them to be one with the inhabitants with which Europe had been long familiar in Southern Asia. But when, nineteen years later, Balboa, looking from the heights of the Isthmus of Darien, discovered a vast ocean extending far to the north and the south and the west, it first became apparent that America was a separate continent. And the people, on further investigation, were pronounced a distinct race or division of the human family.

This at once raised the question whence they came?

Discovery of America.

The generally received opinion that the human family descended from a single pair, found a new complication in this people, so far separated by wide reaches of ocean from the home of the infant race.

Of the various theories advanced, that their progenitors had crossed Behring's Straits from the dreary regions of Siberia, in search of a more genial clime; that they had drifted unwittingly in Chinese junks upon this fair land; that they were degenerate offspring of the Norsemen, who, centuries before, peopled the shores of Greenland, none were entirely satisfactory, for neither of them was capable of proof. Moreover, it afterward appeared that the Indian in different sections of America corresponded to the real or fancied types of nearly all the races, so that all the theories practically failed.

Whence came the Indian?

It is not our purpose now to inquire which of these theories is most plausible, nor to attempt to settle the question as to how long a time the Indian occupied the soil of America before the voyage of the valiant Genoese in 1492.

For while perplexed with this problem we encounter another still more mysterious and remote, and having in it, therefore, more of curious interest, if not the promise of more satisfactory results.

It concerns a race that perished here when the

Indian came, or possibly long before. A race whose mysterious footprints are not hard to trace or difficult of interpretation. And yet a race that long baffled conjecture and almost defied investigation. But we have one or two clues with which to begin.

<small>The earlier race.</small>

The favorite method of preserving the memory of great men and great events, in all times, has been by means of monuments. And the mightiest structures of the world are those erected in memory of the dead, or of events in which human lives were given as the price of conquest or victory. Homer recognizes this general truth, when in his stately verse he makes the valiant Trojan say of his heroic enemy,

<small>Monumental records.</small>

> "The long-haired Greek
> To him upon the shores of Hellespont,
> A mound shall heap! that those in after times
> Who sail along the darksome sea shall say,
> This is the monument of one long since
> Borne to his grave, by mighty Hector slain."

The pyramids of Egypt were long considered but kingly monuments; and if, as now appears, they were built for other uses also, we can only say they served a double purpose, whereof the former was not the least. The practice of building monuments obtained among the early peoples of America no less than with those who built the pyramids, and the custom survives in various forms to-day.

Then, aside from mere memorial structures, the more lasting and distinctive works of every people and every age become in a sense monumental, preserving as they do whatever is peculiar in the life and customs of the times they represent. Herodotus assumes a new significance in the light of Clark's explorations of the tumuli of Scythia. And the romance of Egyptian history becomes reality as we thread the corridors of the labyrinth and explore the recesses of the pyramids.

And in Great Britain, within the historic period, the early diffusion of Celts and Saxons, the intrusions of the Danes, the incursions of the Romans, and the visits of Phœnician traders, are each and all indicated to the educated eye, by walls and roads and heaps of stones, which to the unlettered vision may have no significance.

So, in America, the histories of the earlier ages are, alas, unwritten, save as they may be deciphered in fragments of roads and gardens, in crumbling walls and mounds, and decaying ruins of more elaborate architecture.

Long before the Indians of the present day, there lived, in the interior of North America, a race of men who disappeared centuries ago, leaving no trace of history or even a name behind. From the

REMAINS OF ANCIENT CIVILIZATION. 249

western slope of the Alleghanies, through the Ohio valley, and even beyond the Mississippi, in rarer instances, are found the footprints of this mysterious race.

Their monuments—for so, for convenience, we shall call the relics of their life—take generally the form of mounds. There is no such thing as shaft or obelisk among them. It may be these people had not the skill "to hew the shaft or lay the architrave;" but it is probable, also, that these forms would not have served their intended purposes. *American antiquities.*

Careful observation enables us to divide these structures into three general classes, each having reference to some specific use: the first for war or defence, the second for sacrifice or worship, and the third for the burial of the dead. *Classes of works.*

We present a few examples of the first class.

On the bank of a small stream near Chillicothe, Ohio, the summit of a high hill is occupied by an irregular work of earth and stone of great extent, closely resembling the breastworks used in modern warfare. Its construction indicates that it was intended for defence, while its situation on the brow or summit of a hill, flanked by a running stream, peculiarly adapted it for such purpose. It is not a wall in the strict sense *Defensive works in Ohio.*

of the term, but a line of stones heaped somewhat indiscriminately together, extending around the hill a little below the brow, and rising above the general level at the more exposed points. It shows forecast and calculation much beyond the habit of the modern Indian, and, moreover, indicates an incredible amount of toilsome labor, to which our Indians are specially averse.

It is unreasonable to suppose this work was undertaken for other purposes than warfare or defence; first, because of the position chosen, inconvenient for any other use; and second, because of its immense strength as originally constructed, and the evident intention in making most secure the parts most liable to attack and most difficult to defend.

That this line of fortifications has lost its shape, on the more abrupt side of the hill, is a natural result of the encroachments of time; and that other parts are so lost in debris as to be passed over without observation, is by no means strange when we consider the probable lapse of time since it was constructed. But within a very few years, the entire line could be almost as distinctly traced by a little patient examination of the field, as the lines that engirt the cities of Richmond and Petersburg to-day. This particular enclosure covers an area of more than a hundred acres, and may hence have served as the refuge or rendezvous of a large tribe.

It is even conjectured that they cultivated fields for sustenance within the enclosure, but that could not long have yielded support for any considerable number.

A similar enclosure at Marietta is described as having the additional convenience of a covered way or passage between parallel walls, leading to the Muskingum River near by, that the inmates, in case of siege, might supply themselves with water. There are other enclosures in Ohio covering a much larger extent, and one on the Missouri River, of not less than five hundred acres, which was also provided with a passage-way leading to the river.

On the Miami River, near Hamilton, Ohio, is one of these works—evidently a fortification—more perfect in outline and complete in form, but of less size than that described near Chillicothe. It has four discernible entrances or gateways, the principal one of which is protected by a short curved parapet of similar construction. The chief entrance to one of these enclosures, in Butler County, is defended by a series of curved parapets, both within and without. These structures are simple earthworks, save where stone was abundant, where irregular blocks and boulders were heaped somewhat rudely together without mortar, and were therefore easily displaced.

In a few instances, toward the Gulf of Mexico,

they had sometimes a facing of sun-dried brick (adobe), on which the print of human fingers may still be traced. And to the defensive works so constructed was often added a foss or ditch, sometimes without, but oftener within, the wall. Many of these works are built with considerable mathematical precision ; the usual form being the square, the circle, or the ellipse. Occasionally, as in Pike County, Ohio, there is a square within a circle, though it is by no means certain that these were intended for purposes of defence. When a tribe or nation is driven to the adoption of expedients against an actual or prospective foe, immediate utility counts for more than precision in form or minuteness or detail. Still, the general character of the works is the same as those before described.

Another class of structures closely associated with the foregoing, and belonging essentially with the defensive works, are called "Mounds of Observation," or alarm posts. They are small at the base and higher in proportion, and are found especially in open or level countries, or on elevated points adjoining towns or fortified positions. They may have been rendered necessary by the inimical relations which always subsist between different tribes, even when partially civilized, or may have served as a means of safety against a common foe. They were used probably

[margin: Mounds of observation.]

REMAINS OF ANCIENT CIVILIZATION. 253

both to give notice of approaching danger, and for conveying tidings rapidly to remote points by means of signals.

Similar methods are now employed by the Indians to convey tidings from point to point, though they avail themselves either of the open plain, or of slight natural elevations, instead of erecting mounds at great cost of labor.

Indian signals.

Once when travelling at night in Western Utah, we observed, at intervals, fire signals made from village to village along our line of travel. A bright blaze suddenly started up, and as suddenly disappeared, like the will o' the wisp, as if some tinder-like material had been kindled and immediately smothered, and could therefore be easily distinguished from the light of the wigwam or the camp-fire of the emigrant. This signal appearing at one point was repeated at another, and then another, and so on.

The second general class of these works have been styled *Sacred* enclosures, from their apparent use. They are regular in shape, forming almost a circle, with an opening at one side, or sometimes very like a horseshoe, with a small mound in the centre, which may have served for sacrificial purposes. Unlike the former class in situation, they are found on a plain, some-

Sacred enclosures.

times in a valley, quite indefensible, and therefore utterly unfit for the uses of war. These have been thought to resemble the "ring forts" of the Druids, or ancient Celtic priests, which Cæsar found in Briton, and which were their places of augury and sacrifice.

Indeed, it is claimed that the resemblance of all these works, sacred and defensive, to some of the fortifications of Europe in remote ages, and the sacrificial enclosures of the ancient Celts, is so close as to indicate that they are the work of the same people. But this resemblance is probably purely accidental, or due to the fact that they served like uses in the two cases. Especially in the case of defensive works, similar positions would naturally be selected. A valley with surrounding hills would not be chosen for a fortification, because of the difficulty of defending it; nor a high hill far from running streams, because of the difficulty of supplying it with water. And these simple facts would suggest themselves to any intelligent people, whether in one age and country or another. These considerations, therefore, afford no evidence that the people of Europe and those of ancient America had any knowledge of or relation to one another.

Compared to European.

This explanation of the general form of their sacred enclosures has been suggested: that the people were worshippers of the sun, and there may have been some supposed virtue in conforming their holy places, in shape, to that of the great luminary whence they supposed all life to flow. But this is almost purely conjectural. They may have been sun-worshippers. The other inference does not necessarily follow.

<small>Sun-worshippers.</small>

Little as these works are known to Americans generally, they are as extensive, at one or two points—as at Newark, Ohio,—as those of Stonehenge or Carnac, which are among the most mysterious wonders of England and France to-day. Built generally of earth, however, they have been almost obliterated by the ravages of time, or buried beneath the accretions of overlying soils; great forests, the growth of centuries in many cases, covering the ground they occupied.

Before completing the description of the works, intended for religious uses, we turn to notice another class, between which and the sacred works it is not always easy to distinguish.

These are the *Sepulchral* mounds, in some respects the most important of all these ancient structures, and the ones from which the "mound-builder" really takes his name; though the enclosures give us more of an insight into his mode of life.

<small>Sepulchral mounds.</small>

And here we shall find it necessary to make a careful distinction between the "mound-builders" and the race that came after; a distinction too often disregarded in discussing this subject.

On the borders of Ossipee Lake, New Hampshire, near St. Regis on the St. Lawrence River, on the island of Tonawanda in Niagara River, and at various points in the middle and sea-board States, are heaps of earth a few feet in height and a few rods in extent, small conical or truncated hillocks which are popularly known as "Indian mounds." They are artificial structures, though at a little distance easily mistaken for natural formations; and on examination are found to contain human remains, whence they are known to have been burial-places of the Indians. Sometimes there is an enclosure of earthwork containing several places of sepulture. One of these, a few miles east of Buffalo, is said to contain the remains of Red Jacket, the renowned chief of the Iroquois a century ago.

<small>Indian mounds.</small>

These, however, are all of comparatively recent date, and not the work of the "mound-builders" proper.

According to the elaborate "annals" of the French Jesuits, it was the custom among the Hurons and Iroquois, and perhaps some other tribes, to have at stated intervals—once in seven to ten years—a "festival of the dead," when the remains of such as had died within the period were collected and given a common burial, and a sort of mound erected over them. Such are the works just enumerated. But these are the work of the Indian race that now inhabits, in roving tribes, our western territories, and not of the people with whom we have especially to deal.

These works bear but a crude resemblance to those of the "mound-builders," and may generally be distinguished by their geographical distribution. The lesser works lie chiefly, if not entirely, to the eastward of the great lakes and the Alleghany Mountains; those of the "mound-builders," with very rare exceptions, lie to the westward of the Alleghanies.

Distribution of mounds.

We now return to a consideration of the sepulchral mounds.

At Grave Creek, West Virginia, is one of the most remarkable of this class. It is seventy feet in height, and not less than nine hundred feet in circumference at the base. About forty years ago this mound was opened and explored. A drift or tunnel was made at the base toward the centre, and a shaft sunk from the top to intercept it. About forty feet from the summit the workmen came upon a vault about eight by twelve feet, and seven feet in

Grave Creek mound

height, formed by supporting timbers at the sides and overhead. And at the base of the mound was another chamber reached both by the shaft from above and the drift from without; somewhat larger than the first, but of similar construction. In each of these vaults was found the skeleton of a human being, surrounded with such a wealth of ornaments, especially the beads and shells prized by primitive people for decoration, as to leave little doubt that they were the skeletons of chiefs or kings. In the lower vault was found also another skeleton near the first but without ornament, suggesting the idea that it may have been an attendant to whom it was considered honor enough to be buried with the king. Further examination discovered other remains disposed about the tomb a few feet from the central figure, and with these was mingled charcoal, while the bones showed marks of burning.

These somewhat startling facts call up vividly the account of the burial of the Scythian kings, as detailed by the old Greek historian.

When the king was dead, the body was placed in a tomb prepared for the purpose; one of his concubines was strangled and the body burned in close proximity to the royal personage; then the cook, cup-bearer, groom, messenger and horse were sacrificed immediately around the tomb and the whole concealed beneath an imposing mound.

We may not be warranted as yet, perhaps, in assuming that such ghastly funeral rites prevailed among the ancient peoples of America, but these revelations seem to point in that direction. *Possible human sacrifices.*

Prof. O. C. Marsh, of New Haven, describes a mound he explored in 1865, near Newark, Ohio, about ten feet high and eighty feet in circumference, which was overgrown with forest trees, some of them more than six feet in diameter. *Discoveries of Prof. Marsh.*

The excavation was made from the apex downward and revealed several series of skeletons at different depths below the surface. First were the remains of a child with a string of copper beads about the neck. About one foot below were two skeletons, a male and a female, carefully enclosed in layers of bark, above which were charred remnants of other skeletons which suggested the possibility that the latter had been sacrificed, made a burnt offering, in honor of the others. At a greater depth were found still other remains, generally much decayed, which seems to indicate that a single structure was made to answer the purpose of several successive burials. In this mound were found several hatchets of hematite and greenstone, a flint chisel, needles made from the small bones in a deer's foot, a few bits of pottery and bones of animals. Other mounds of this class on being opened disclosed similar contents, so that further descriptions of them are unnecessary.

Some of these mounds have been opened in more recent times, and used as burial-places by the Indians. It is even conjectured that the Indian cemeteries described in Western New York were originally the work of the "mound-builder," afterward appropriated by the Indians. But these intrusions upon the sanctity of the ancient sepulchre are easily detected, as the regular strata so carefully laid by the original builders are disturbed and the symmetry of the structure therefore impaired.

<small>Intrusion of Indians.</small>

There is another class of these works, known as *Temple mounds*. They have the form of a truncated pyramid, and are supposed to have served as foundations for temples, which being built of wood or other perishable material have utterly disappeared.

<small>Temple mounds.</small>

Chief among these is, or was, the great mound at Cahokia, Illinois, ninety feet in height, with a rectangular base five hundred by seven hundred feet. There was a broad terrace reached by a graded way on one side, and the summit of the mound was two hundred by four hundred and fifty feet. Mr. Foster, in his prehistoric races, speaking of this mound, gives his imagination wings as fol lows: "It is probable that upon this platform was reared a capacious temple, within whose walls the high priests gathered from different quarters at stated seasons, celebrating their mystic rites, while the swarming multitude below looked up with mute adoration." The suggestion is taken from the similarity of these mounds to the bases of religious edifices in Mexico and Yucatan. There are smaller structures of the same class as the Cahokia mound in various parts of the country, and supposed to have served the same purposes.

There are yet other classes of mounds to which no specific use can be assigned. They seem to represent some fantastic conceit, since they take the forms of animals— the fox, the bear, the turtle with tail of extraordinary length, or buffaloes in procession. These are especially numerous in Wisconsin; one on Fox River represents the outlines of a bird; one near Baraboo takes the form of a man; one in Mississippi the bust of a woman; and one elaborate structure in Adams County, Ohio, has the shape of a serpent with a triple coil at the tail. One or two have been described bearing some resemblance to the elephant or mastodon. Whether these were mere idle conceits; whether they were regarded only as triumphs of art or invention, or whether they represented the ideal conceptions

Animal mounds.

of their religion, as the Gods of the Egyptians took the forms of animals and men, is matter as yet of pure conjecture.

Of far more interest, however, than the mounds themselves, whatever their form, are the contents found in them. These are the real memorials of the people, since they indicate the degree of civilization they had attained, by the knowledge of art which they possessed.

<small>Works of art and industry.</small>

Wrought copper is found in considerable quantities, whence we infer that they understood mining and had some knowledge of metallurgy; marine shells are also found in some of the mounds far in the interior, whence we conclude they had some sort of communication, or commercial intercourse with the sea.

They had axes and ornaments of the hardest stone, so smoothly and skilfully wrought, we must suppose they had some knowledge of the more difficult mechanic arts. While their pipes and pottery were often wrought with such precision, and such fidelity to nature in the forms they represent, as to entitle them to the name of artists, as well as artizans. They spun thread and made woven fabrics.

Several tablets, with mystic engravings have been reported from the mounds from time to time;

but their genuineness is doubted. And though the horse was probably unknown in America at that day, there is evidence that they moved from place to place with considerable facility, and so must have had convenient means of transportation.

Inasmuch as fragments of copper have been found in the glacial drift all over the western States, south of the Lake Superior region, it was long supposed that this may have been the "mound-builders" source of supply. Recent investigations, however, have led to a different conclusion.

Mr. Knapp, the Superintendent of the Lake Superior mines, in 1848, discovered an old shaft twenty-six feet deep, which was filled to the depth of about twenty feet with mingled clay and mouldering vegetation. *The "mound-builders" mined copper.* At this depth he came upon a mass of copper, of about six tons weight, which had been raised five feet from its original bed and rested on a framework of oak timbers. The miners seem to have raised it to this height and then abandoned it. The wood quickly crumbled on exposure to the air, but the earth was so closely packed about the mass as to hold it in position after the under support was gone. About this was found a number of stone hammers, mostly of porphyry, also mauls or sledge-hammers, both of stone and copper, with copper wedges used probably in moving the heavy weight upon the wooden supports. Upon the debris of another shaft in the same vicinity was found a tree still growing, which on examination proved to be about four hundred years old, while the crumbling remains of earlier generations lay across the pit.

Nor were these isolated cases. Wherever the mining regions of Lake Superior have been explored, either on the islands or on the southern shore, are found the traces of this ancient race. And as there are no evidences of permanent abodes, as in the warmer regions toward the south, the inference follows that they visited and worked these mines only in the summer, and therefore must have had means of going to and fro at least with moderate speed.

It has been stated that in the oil regions of Ohio or Pennsylvania, there are wells of such remote construction as to warrant the belief that they were the work of the "mound-builders." We have never been able to trace a case of the kind with sufficient certainty to warrant an opinion on the subject. If, however, they worked our mines and practised our arts so long before ourselves, it is by no means impossible that they were equally in advance of us in the production and use of oil.

Did they dig oil wells?

Having now described, with sufficient detail for

our purpose, the different classes of mounds, with the uses they served and the treasures they reveal, we pass to the important inquiry—

How old are these mounds?

It is a difficult question, but we have some data from which to form an opinion.

The atmosphere of this country is drier and more favorable for the preservation of the dead than that of Great Britain. But the remains found in the mounds of this country are more decayed than those in the Celtic mounds found by Cæsar at the time of his invasion of those islands. So the American mounds seem to antedate the Roman conquest of Britain, which took place a half century before the birth of Christ; that is, the mounds are hardly less, and may be more than two thousand years old.

<small>Evidence of antiquity.</small>

This, of course, supposes them to be the work of a race long preceding the Indians. But there are two or three facts independent of the foregoing considerations, that go far to establish this theory:

1. They were not nomadic tribes. Had they been, instead of building fortifications that were to stand for ages, they would have moved from place to place, as the necessities of the situation required.

2. They were an agricultural people. For no people living in permanent settlements can long depend for a living on the precarious returns of

the chase. And even their sepulchral mounds indicate the established character of their habitations, since they must have been long years in building.

3. There is indisputable evidence that the works were not only built but abandoned centuries ago. Over the excavated mines of Lake Superior, as already stated, were found trees of more than four hundred years growth. On the mound at Grave Creek were trees nearly seven hundred years old, while on one on the Muskingum River was a tree presumed to be not less than eight hundred years of age. These must all have grown after the works were abandoned, to say nothing of the fact that the original forest trees are not the first to reappear, after being once displaced.

These considerations carry us back not less than a thousand years, and the period may be much greater. No definite date can be fixed.

Who, then, were the " mound-builders ? "

Some will answer, a peculiar race of whom the present Indian is the degenerate offspring. Others will say, a band of Aztecs from Mexico, who made incursions into these northern latitudes till driven thence by other tribes, or who returned at will to their former country leaving these traces behind; and others still place them outside the pale of all recorded history.

Various theories.

Neither of these theories seem to be well founded.

To suppose these mound-builders to have been the progenitors of the Indians is to place them back anywhere from three hundred to five hundred years. But the Indians have no record of them; nothing more than a faint tradition, and that apparently founded on the mounds themselves; to say nothing of the utter dissimilarity between them in character, government, habits, and modes of life.

The fact that no mounds are found on the lower river terraces, the last in the series of terraces formed after the close of the glacial period, has led some to conclude that the mounds were built before the close of the terrace epoch. We see no sufficient reason for such conclusion. The fact itself, however, is of less importance than may at first appear; for even at the present day the lower terraces are subject to overflow, and not, therefore, safe for earthworks of any kind. Besides, for almost every purpose the mounds are supposed to have served, the higher ground was better. *No mounds on river terraces.*

As to the remaining theory, based on similarity of arts and wares, that the "mound-builders" were descendants of the Aztecs, or possibly of the Toltecs, of Central America; or rather that the mounds were the work of one *Relation to Aztecs.*

or the other of these nations out on a sort of holiday excursion, it is sufficient to say that excursionists do not build elaborate fortifications, much less construct defences that will last for centuries, even if the exigencies compel them to throw up hasty breastworks, as a defence against an unexpected foe. Nor does the supposition that they were temporary colonies sent out merely for experiment make the case more probable.

Besides, no well authenticated record or inscription of the Toltecs in Nicaragua dates back beyond the sixth or probably the seventh century, and the Aztecs come some four hundred years later. In other words, trees found still growing on the mounds in Ohio, date back even with the earliest known existence of the Aztecs in Mexico; that is, the mounds were completed and *abandoned* before the existence of the Aztecs as a nation.

<small>Record of Toltecs.</small>

But if a similarity in art and architecture argues a connection between the "mound-builder" and these Southern peoples, why not suppose the Aztecs to have descended from the "mound-builders" instead of the reverse? Certain it is, that so far as we have any data on which to form an opinion, the latter were the older or earlier race.

A consideration of all the facts bearing upon the subject lead us to the following hypothesis.

Two thousand years ago, more or less, the interior of this continent was occupied by a large population of semi-civilized men far surpassing the Indian of a later day. Whence they came it is little better than idle, at the present stage of investigation, to inquire. That is a problem that cannot yet be solved, if it ever shall be. After having been long established in permanent abodes, they were driven from their homes by the incursion of powerful northern or eastern tribes, like that of Alaric and his hosts, that came down upon Rome fourteen hundred years ago, leaving behind in these mounds the evidence of their civil condition and modes of life. As they withdrew toward the south-west they made temporary stands, here and there, and erected some of their characteristic works, till, driven thence, they crossed the broad reaches of Texas and found a retreat in Mexico. And there, under more favoring circumstances, they developed the type of civilization that culminated in the halls and courts of Montezuma.

A hypothesis.

Our reason for supposing the "mound-builders" to so far antedate the Aztecs is, that the latter were at the height of their civilization, or perhaps in its early decline, when Cortez invaded their country in the sixteenth century, while the latest known work of the former carries us well back toward the beginning of the Christian Era, or possibly beyond it.

One more question remains to be considered, *What finally became of the "mound-builders?"*

It is unreasonable to suppose such a people could have perished utterly, even after the disasters of the Spanish campaign in Mexico, or that they could have been so entirely absorbed by other nations as to leave no characteristic traces of themselves.

From the reports of explorers and surveying parties, we have become somewhat familiar in recent years with what are known as the Pueblo Indians of New Mexico and Arizona, and also to a limited extent with the Cliff-dwellers. This region, especially Arizona, is largely a desert country, but with frequent oases of considerable extent and fertility. It is apparent that the country has un dergone important geologic and perhaps climatic changes in the past few centuries, by which its area of fertile lands has been considerably reduced; and this has tended more and more to isolate its inhabitants from the outside world; so that for a long period almost nothing was known of them. Recently it has come to light, however, that at various points in this region are towns or communities of people, in many respects unlike both the whites and the Indians. They are mild in disposition and have some habits of industry. They have many of the arts of civilized life, though evidently degenerated from what they once were. They keep sheep, spin and weave, and clothe themselves, in part, in textile fabrics. And they cultivate fields, though by rude and comparatively inefficient means.

Some of them are Pueblo Indians and some of them Cliff-dwellers. The former have great buildings, large enough to accommodate a whole community; sometimes of concrete or adobe, and sometimes of stone, where that material can be readily obtained. They are often several stories in height, each story receding from the one next below, giving it much the appearance, as Lieutenant Whipple describes it, of a huge ant-hill; which appearance is much heightened by the passing in and out of the busy multitude. There are no doors or gateways in the lower story, the only access being by ladders reaching to one of the upper terraces. These buildings are all of ancient date. Most of them are in ruins, but a few are still kept in a moderate state of repair. *Pueblo Indians.*

The Cliff-dwellers perch like swallows on summits or in niches of the eroded rocks. They were, by their own account, driven to this extremity many years ago, by relentless foes who gave them no rest and allowed *Cliff-dwellers.*

them no safe retreat. Their houses, even in these precarious positions, are built and furnished with moderate skill and comfort, though the access to them, sometimes from the summit above and sometimes from the canyon beneath, is difficult and often hazardous.

The people most remotely and completely separated from the rest of the world are known as the Moquis, and there are reported six or seven considerable communities of them. There may be more, for the territory is not yet completely explored. Their extreme isolation from the world, by the desert regions round about, have shielded them now for centuries past, from the assaults of savage tribes on the one hand, and the encroachments of modern civilization on the other. Of the domestic affairs of these people, little is known, as they do not court investigation.

The Moquis.

Prof. Newberry, of Columbia College, paid them a brief visit a few years ago, and gives us some interesting facts concerning them. Approaching one of their towns, he saw first a group of girls or young women tending a flock of sheep, showing them to be a pastoral people and suggesting patriarchal times. The houses were such as have been described. In the morning it is their habit to go upon the house-top and do obeisance to the rising

REMAINS OF ANCIENT CIVILIZATION. 273

sun, a remnant certainly, if not a form of worship of the sun. After the manner of the ancient Greeks, they recognize deities or guardian spirits as presiding over fountains and the like. Coming to a spring on their journeys, they make an offering before they drink. A handful of meal scattered about the fountain may serve the purpose. They suspend something like a piece of candle-wick with one end in the spring, and when the water, following the law of capillary attraction, runs up the wick, they account it evidence that the spirit is drinking, that their offering is accepted and they are at liberty to drink.

Who, now, are these people, and whence came they?

Again we answer for ourselves.

They are the feeble remnant of the Aztecs—the mighty people, mighty at least in numbers, who under the Montezumas held the vast rich fields of Mexico, till they fell before the cupidity of the Spanish conqueror. And if the Aztecs were the "mound-builders" and the Moquis were the Aztecs, the deduction is a plain one, that the Moquis of New Mexico to-day, are the remote remnant of the "mound-builders" of the Mississippi valley of two thousand years ago.

The "mound-builders" and the Moquis.

We shall be met at this point by some enthusiastic archæologists whose opinion is entitled to respect, with the assumption that there is no similarity between the languages of these two races, so remote from one another. But they will probably insist on some connection between the "mound-builders" and the Aztecs.

<small>Language of the "mound-builders."</small>

We reply, that of the language of the "mound-builders" we know absolutely nothing. And it is, therefore, as impossible to trace any affinity in language between the "mound-builders" and the Aztecs, as between the "mound-builders" and the Moquis. But there is a likeness in art and architecture, in apparent religion and modes of life, between the "mound-builders" and the Aztecs, and a still better established likeness between the Aztecs and the Moquis.

We have little data on which to trace the ethnic relations of the "mound-builders."

In two or three skulls recovered in a sufficient state of preservation to be accurately examined, is the low forehead and prominent cheek-bone, that suggest the Mongolian rather than the Caucasian race, and yet it is not established that they belonged to either. Judged by these skulls, they were not given to great virtues or great vices; nor were they great inventors, though probably clever imitators; a mild and comparatively inoffensive race; capable of efficient service under

<small>Race affinities.</small>

a master mind, but falling an easy prey to a crafty and cruel foe. Such a people might be efficient in building the Chinese wall, or the Egyptian pyramids, or the mounds of the great West, but are not likely to achieve great success in life. These qualities were evident characteristics of the "mound-builders." They are historic characteristics of the Aztecs; and from what we have been able to learn, are the actual and present characteristics of the Moquis.

This, then, is an epitome of the whole matter. The "mound-builders" inhabited the valleys of the Mississippi and its tributaries not less than two thousand years ago. They were a peculiar people, unlike the whites and unlike the Indians of recent times. They possessed a good degree of civilization; lived in fixed communities, cultivated fields, and clothed themselves in fabrics woven by their own hands. They modelled images in clay, carved the hardest stone, and erected elaborate defences against a foe. They had a national religion, built temples and altars, and offered sacrifices. They had also a stable government, in which the masses were subordinate to the ruling power.

<small>Epitome and conclusion.</small>

Driven out at length from their established homes, they withdrew toward the south-west, into Mexico, and possibly into Nicaragua, where they practiced the same arts as before, their architecture assuming an improved and more lasting form.

Finally, overrun and driven again from home, they withdrew toward the North, gradually dwindling in numbers and declining in enterprise by reason of their multiplied ill-fortunes. And now, in the midst of a comparatively desert region are the remains of the second empire—the power that after the mound-builders held dominion and left traces of civilization in North America.

THE END

www.ingramcontent.com/pod-product-compliance
Lightning Source LLC
Chambersburg PA
CBHW052214240426
43670CB00037B/443